Fun *in* Sobriety

AAGRAPEVINE, Inc.

New York, New York
WWW. AAGRAPEVINE.ORG

Fun
in
Sobriety

How AA members learn to live sober
and enjoy life to its fullest

AAGRAPEVINE,Inc.
New York, New York
WWW. AAGRAPEVINE.ORG

AA Preamble

Alcoholics Anonymous is a fellowship of people
who share their experience, strength and hope with each
other that they may solve their common problem
and help others to recover from alcoholism.

The only requirement for membership is a desire to stop drinking.
There are no dues or fees for AA membership;
we are self-supporting through our own contributions.
AA is not allied with any sect, denomination, politics, organization
or institution; does not wish to engage in any controversy,
neither endorses nor opposes any causes.

Our primary purpose is to stay sober
and help other alcoholics to achieve sobriety.

Contents

CHAPTER ONE

Adventures With the Fellowship

Home groups, conventions and get-togethers—having a great time with other sober members

CHAPTER TWO

Creative Dreams Come Alive

Painting, singing, dancing and more—life gets busy when we put down the bottle

CHAPTER THREE

Living It Up

Having sober fun at concerts, parties and social events

CHAPTER FOUR

The Great & Glorious Outdoors

Hiking, swimming and horseback riding—enjoying some fresh air and a good sober time

CHAPTER FIVE

Going Places

Planes, trains, ships and laptops—traveling the globe without a drink

Welcome

"We aren't a glum lot. If newcomers could see no joy or fun in our existence, they wouldn't want it. We absolutely insist on enjoying life."
—*AA cofounder Bill. W.*, Alcoholics Anonymous

People seeking sobriety who come to an AA meeting for the first time may expect many things—an introduction to the AA program, a helping hand, a cup of coffee—but they are often surprised by the laughter they hear. After all, getting sober is serious, life-saving business. How can people be having so much fun?

The personal stories in *Fun in Sobriety* describe how, freed from alcohol, people can and do live life to its fullest. In a sense, this book could serve as a primer for newly recovering alcoholics who find themselves awakening to a new morning and a day filled with possibility. The stories inside describe AA members connecting with each other through the Fellowship, to attend meetings or travel together to AA events, picnics and holiday celebrations, forming bonds of friendship that last a lifetime. Chapters feature stories about enjoying life with fellow AA members, discovering creativity, having fun at concerts and social events, exploring the outdoors and traveling to faraway places— all without drinking.

Part of having fun in sobriety is rediscovering talents that have lain dormant. People literally learn how to dance again ("You just make up your mind to do it," says the writer of Chapter Two's "Dancing Machine"), to draw, to paint, to write, to play music, to cook a fabulous meal. Travel, which had previously been fraught with fears of blackouts in strange places, lost tickets and misspent funds, is now a way to explore new horizons in sobriety. The same goes for outdoor activities like sports, camping, tubing and bowling.

Kay K., whose story "Party Girl" is in Chapter Three, has been sober more than two decades. As an AA newcomer, she "saw an utterly flat landscape ahead—no drinking, and also no parties and no fun. I couldn't imagine what form of faith these people had that was sustaining them and their happy smiles while having no enjoyment in life whatsoever. What could they possibly have to look forward to?"

Everything, she discovers. Sobriety isn't always easy, but laughter—and fun in all its forms—is one of the many rewards of a life in the AA Fellowship.

CHAPTER ONE

Adventures With the Fellowship

Home groups, conventions and get-togethers—having a great time with other sober members

---

The stories in this chapter illustrate the genuine pleasure sober alcoholics find in connecting through AA meetings, conferences, alcathons, holiday potlucks—anyplace where alcoholics gather to stay sober and help other alcoholics.

Meetings are often the first places new AAs find where sobriety can be a joyful experience. In her story, "The Rowdiest, Rockingest Group," Gwyneth N. describes herself as a "sofa drunk" whose idea of a good time was "getting into bed with a tumblerful of wine and an old paperback." She certainly didn't expect to find laughter in the "dingy basement" of a church. But six years into sobriety, the meetings of her Maine home group became a source of friendship and deep satisfaction. As Dossie P. puts it in "Where the Party Is," "there is no entertainment comparable to a jolly AA meeting. No television, no movie, no live theater will leave you walking out the door with the feeling of joy and well-being that a good meeting brings."

Service is a tried-and-true path to connection in AA. "Be of service wherever you are" is K.W.'s mantra. In "Butterflies at the Alcathon," she steps into a holiday gathering of fellow alcoholics and feeling a little nervous at the size of the crowd, makes a beeline to help at the food tables. Handing out cookies, making small talk—in welcoming others, she welcomes herself. In "Two Free Hands," newcomer Jenni C. joins the host committee for her first conference of Young People in AA, and with her friends at her side, "showed other young AAs that you can have fun in sobriety."

Because AA is, well, AA, there are myriad ways to enjoy yourself at meetings and events. "Ever dream you were...in an AA meeting naked as a jaybird?" is the hilarious opening to "A Nude Awakening," the 1990 story of a nudist meeting held amidst towering Douglas firs in the Oregon wilderness. Despite its unusual circumstances, member David W. writes, "the real idea of all this is to show you that AA is indeed everywhere." In the tale "Twisted Sisters," Denise R. extolls her California home group, a women's meeting where "we women have found a way out and a way of life that has truly rocketed us into the Fourth Dimension. Please come by and visit!"

Even if you are unable to visit the Twisted Sisters—or prefer not to shed your clothes for an AA meeting!—you'll enjoy yourself vicariously as you read about the endless ways people enjoy life and sobriety at AA events. As the Big Book says: "Why shouldn't we laugh? We have recovered, and have been given the power to help others."

The Rowdiest, Rockingest Group
October 2004

When people think about fun in sobriety, their thoughts often go to sober bowling, hanging out at the local diner, drinking bad coffee or dancing the night away at a Fellowship dance. For me, the most fun I have in sobriety is right here at my Saturday night meeting, surrounded by old friends and experiencing the joy of welcoming a newcomer. What could be more fun?

I never danced on tables or trashed hotel rooms. I was a "sofa drunk." I never came to in a strange country surrounded by empty bottles of tequila. I never stole a car, a tractor, a snowmobile or a farm animal while in a blackout. And I never drank anybody under a table.

I was the mom who drank. I was the wife and teacher who drank. And I did it very quietly. Every day and every night I drank, and those days and nights stretched into years—years when my children grew up and my marriage grew strained and my career stagnated—all unnoticed by me.

Back then, my idea of fun was drawing the blinds and getting into bed with a tumblerful of wine and an old paperback.

When I hear people talk about all the crazy adventures they had while drinking, I can't really relate. Aside from a few moments in college (I vaguely remember singing Patsy Cline on the hood of a car) drinking wasn't linked to fun. Alcohol was soothing. It allowed me to handle the stress and anxiety of being a mom and working full-time as a middle-school teacher.

Most of all, alcohol provided me with obliteration. The traumas of my childhood were forgotten the moment I had that first sip of chardonnay. It shut down the incessant chatter in my head and let me feel some peace.

So I never expected AA would be fun. How could it be? I figured the Fellowship would be filled with grumpy old men with coffee-stained teeth and their sullen, disappointed wives. I didn't have any fun while I was drinking and I resigned myself to the fact that I wouldn't have fun in sobriety either.

It may come as a bit of a shock then, that I managed to pick the rowdiest, wildest, rockingest home group in the entire state of Maine: The Old Orchard Beach Beginners' Meeting—known to everyone from around these parts as "The Greatest Group in the Galaxy." It sometimes feels more like a big family reunion than an AA meeting, especially in the summer when all our friends "from away" come in.

When I first walked into our meeting hall back in 2009, I was struck by the wall of sound. It wasn't just laughter, but guffawing, knee-slapping laughter, the kind you can't help but laugh along with. Believe me, it had been a long time since I'd found a reason to laugh. I certainly didn't expect to find laughter in the dingy basement of a Methodist church.

The next thing that happened was the warm greeting I got, yelled at top volume along with a vigorous handshake and smile. "Welcome," my new friends said. "You're in the right place."

That first AA meeting is a bit of a blur now. What I remember most is the energy of the pre-meeting, the coming together of such disparate fellows to celebrate life. I remember too the shock of the first clap of the gavel, followed by instantaneous silence and the sweet sound of the Serenity Prayer. Even today, that sudden shift from cacophony to calm fills me with gratitude for the special place I call my home group.

As it happens, sobriety has been a whole lot more fun than drinking was. My life has become so much richer and fuller in the six years since I got sober. I no longer crave obliteration. I've learned that being fully aware and connected to others is the key to enjoying life.

I've been to lots of sober parties and dances, mostly with women from my home group. I've gone to picnics and sober round-ups. I've gone hiking and spent days at the beach with the new friends I've made in AA. And I've even been to a wedding in AA.

But honestly, the most fun of all is spending Saturday nights with the men and women from The Greatest Group in the Galaxy, the people who loved me and guided me in my early days, the people who continue to support me, challenge me, and help me live each day happy, joyous and free.

Gwyneth N.
Saco, Maine

Spaghetti Legs
August 2018

L et's keep it real. As far as what was considered fun when we were out there, I'll have to agree with my old "homies" when they say, "The only trouble with trouble is that it always starts out as fun." Ain't that the truth?

I can remember how I used to show up to an evening party all clean and pressed with a six pack of beer and some limes (as if to imply that I was bringing them to share). Then sometime during the following 24 hours, I'd find myself facedown in the back of a cop car, or in a motel room with some crazy person on crack, or possibly whacked out on PCP and up in a tree, or some other type of "fun" like that.

Once I came into the rooms, I looked around and saw the low-low bottoms, then the low bottoms, and lastly, a variety of high bottoms. Some people who, with no reservation, would talk about how much fun they had when they were out there. These individuals would usually preface their shares with some kind of obligatory, "I ain't gonna lie" line, as if this made having fun forgivable.

I did think that once I got sober, life was entirely over, apart from meetings and work. I can remember hearing that wonderful saying, "You need to change one thing about your life and that's everything." I sincerely envisioned myself sitting in a chair in the middle of my room doing nothing.

Someone pointed out that I lived in a world in which my friends drank and used, my roommates drank and used, my boss was my speed connection, and I lived in the "hood." People told me I needed to change my play friends, my playthings, and my playgrounds.

And just as I was starting to think I would never have any fun in my life again, I was talking one Saturday evening after a meeting with members gathered around in the parking lot. "We're going bowling," someone yelled.

I thought, Wait. Cool people don't bowl. And then instantly a few memories came rushing forward. I remembered my old kind of fun, which often ended with a field sobriety test. So I got in the car and off we went to the bowling alley.

There we were, beggars, tramps, asylum inmates, drunks, prisoners and plain crackpots. And we were bowling, and it was awesome. It was The Longest Yard and Bad News Bears go bowling!

The next weekend, we had a dance. I showed up proudly flying my neighborhood colors (I didn't know better at the time). We reminded each other to check our egos at the door, as we were almost positive that none of us had ever danced on the "natch" (natural and sober). We geeked out for hours and had the time of our lives.

After these two experiences, I made a promise to God that I would live like I was dying. I would begin to make playing and having fun priorities in my life. Prior to recovery, I was dying, killing myself on the installment plan, and doing nothing else. Now I was sober and enjoying life.

One afternoon, not too long after that dance, I was at a meeting and a buddy of mine closed it with the Lord's Prayer and an invite to everyone there to go water-skiing! That day, he taught a handful of hoodlums like me a wonderful lesson in joy. I remember being so excited to stand up on the skis on my first try. After that, I just kept skiing and skiing. My friend warned me to go easy, that my legs weren't used to this stress. But I was so happy and excited that I didn't listen. I couldn't walk for a week. My legs were like spaghetti.

In the town where I got sober, there were a lot of musicians in recovery and they played in shows almost every week. After meetings, we would caravan out and take the clubs by storm. The waitresses didn't know what to make of us. On one hand, we were a huge, well-mannered crowd. On the other hand we all drank coffee and many of us were near-broke. We would crack a lot of "broke newcomer" jokes. It was hilarious. But we were creating new traditions and new sober memories every week.

My wife, who is also my best friend, is sober too, and over the years we have taken our kids to AA picnics, powwows, camping trips, parties, pig roasts and holiday celebrations. We've also held campfire potluck meetings at our home. There are no friends like those with whom we have shared a common peril. I tell you, we are certainly not a glum lot.

Anonymous
Haskell, Oklahoma

The speaker at the Convention's Big Meeting on Friday night walked up to the podium, looked out at the stadium full of people and said, "My heart is beating, my knees are weak, my stomach is in knots. I used to pay a lot of money for this feeling."
October 2000
Christine H., Michigan

Butterflies at the Alcathon
December 2020

My heart is pounding because I feel uncomfortable at our sober holiday alcathon. And yet I feel an intense need to do service work to anchor my nerves. I am acting on what I've been taught: Be of service wherever you are—it works every time. I know this to be true.

In early sobriety, my sponsor used to tell me, "When you're at a party and you're feeling nervous, go to the kitchen and help out. This will give you something to do. You will be helpful and you'll probably meet people you like. It's 'good orderly direction,' it'll keep your nerves in check, and will help you feel like you belong."

Tonight, as with so many other times in sobriety, I just follow my sponsor's suggestion. I walk around to the back of the long food tables, clean up empty cookie wrappers, brush crumbs into the waste container, throw paper plates away. I use a napkin to add more cookies to the half-full platters. I try to keep it looking inviting and festive for the crowd that's here tonight. In this way, I calm down.

I'm glad to be at a sober holiday event. I thank my Higher Power that my legs have quit shaking and that my heart has slowed its beat. My hands are steady.

Someone asks me for another napkin. Someone needs a glass of water and directions to the bathroom. Another member wants to know where marathon meetings are held. I offer a smile and small talk with the people coming to look over the sweets, fruits, sandwiches and offerings at the tables. Some are just as nervous to be there as I am, ready to run out the door with even the slightest nudge. We connect and I welcome them, giving them a cup for juice or coffee.

The decorations have been out all day and this evening they look a bit haggard, just like I did at the end of big parties in my drinking days. They are a bit lopsided, ruffled from too many falls on the floor. At the end of my time drinking, I was a waitress at a bar. I worked and served drinks in a full blackout. I know I worked on the holidays, but I don't quite remember much about them, except I was always getting fired afterward.

Now it's time for the main speaker to come on. I finish cleaning up, go to my chair up front of the large auditorium and sit with my sponsor. The committee chairperson goes to the podium and speaks into the microphone, welcoming everyone and opening the meeting with the Serenity Prayer. I say it with deep feeling tonight.

A newcomer, with voice shaking, reads Chapter 5, and someone from the sponsoring home group reads the Traditions. Then the chairperson comes back to the podium and announces that it is time for the main speaker. She looks down at me, smiles and calls out my name.

K.W.
Tucson, Arizona

A Nude Awakening
March 1990

Ever dream you were in a restaurant and had no clothes on? Or that you were in an AA meeting naked as a jaybird? Well, for us fortunate recovering alcoholics at a nudist camp ensconced amid the magnificent Douglas firs of the Oregon forest, it is not a dream; it's a reality.

Welcome to the Nude Beginnings meeting of Alcoholics Anonymous. My name is David, and I'm an alcoholic. I am also, among other things, a nudist and a chef.

When it came time for me to semi-retire, it was only natural (a little joke there) that I should semi-retire from the world of textiles (clothes, to you) and live permanently and year-round in a nudist park. I found one near Tucson, Arizona where I could spend the long winter months, and one near Eugene, Oregon where I could enjoy the summer. The camp in Oregon also needed someone to operate its small restaurant on weekends. What could be better for a semi-retired chef?

But before I even opened the front door of the cafe (now known as David's Bistro-in-the-Buff), I hung two beautifully done plaques near the cash register, where everyone could see them. One said "Live and Let Live," and the other said "Happy, Joyous, and Free." Near the exit door, appropriately enough, I placed a third message which proclaimed, "Keep Coming Back." The signs mean something to nonalcoholics, too, of course, but the real joy comes when an AA member spots them, surmises just who might have put them up and discreetly asks me, "Are you a friend of Bill W.?"

However, the greatest thing these proverbs did was to bring enough of us AA folk together so that we could have our very own AA meeting right here in camp.

On Saturday evening the restaurant closes at 6 o'clock. The crew puts things away, finishes the clean-up work, makes fresh coffee, and at 7:30 we open the doors again for the meeting.

It is an open meeting closely patterned after the 7 A.M. Attitude Adjustment Hour in Palm Desert, California—the meeting that got me sober and saved my life. We try to maintain an upbeat, positive exchange right smack in the middle of now.

There were four of us at our first gathering: Betty with 31 years, Roy with 20, Robin with five, and me with nine. So great was our joy at what we were doing that faces beamed, eyes sparkled, and laughter abounded. It was a pretty giddy affair. Then as Sue and Patsy and Keith heard about our meetings and came in, the excitement started all over. Sue celebrated her first birthday with us, Patsy her sixth, and Betty's daughter Michelle, who had also joined us, celebrated her fifth. Two nonalcoholic visitors attend regularly, as does a member of Al-Anon. And because we are primarily a summer resort with many visitors, we get AA people who are here for only a weekend or so.

We're not sure what will happen come October or November, because the chilly rains of the Oregon winter are not too conducive to running around outside in the altogether. Camp business declines drastically, the restaurant goes into hibernation, and some of us leave for sunnier, if not greener, pastures. Nevertheless, you can rest assured the AA slogans will remain in the boarded up Bistro-in-the-Buff, and come springtime, we will return and some trusted servant will again be intoning those magical words, "Welcome to the Nude Beginnings meeting of Alcoholics Anonymous. My name is___, and I am an alcoholic."

The real idea of all this is to show you that AA is indeed everywhere. Next year we plan on having a midnight meeting in the hot tub—as soon as we can find a waterproof Big Book!

So come visit us.

Come celebrate your birthday.

And wear your birthday suit.

David W.
Marana, Arizona

Twisted Sisters
April 2021

I love my home group. We meet on Wednesday nights at 7:00 in a cozy little room next to a little white church in Soquel, California, two miles inland from beautiful Capitola Village.

We read the Spiritual Experience appendix in the back of the Big Book to start us off, read a section and then we all share by candlelight. There are some pretty amazing sober women in this group. It's a very intimate meeting and good times as well as hard times are shared. There's so much support here; we know we can count on each other.

When I got sick and tired of being sick and tired and decided to come into AA, I just followed the footsteps of two very special people in my life. They were already sober, and we had all drunk together, so I decided "if they could do it, I can do it." Thank God for these examples.

Right away, I hooked into a women's meeting in Aptos and met some awesome sober women. One of the women asked me to come to a brand-new meeting (which didn't even have a name yet), so I showed up and worked it into my Wednesday night schedule. They were trying to think of a name. One of the ladies had been on a retreat and a priest had made a comment about his nun friends by lovingly calling them his "twisted sisters." We all looked at each other and said, "That's it!"

That was 23 long years ago and our Twisted Sisters AA meeting is still going strong. We get a lot of out-of-towners coming just because they see our name listed in the local AA meeting schedule. Visitors relate to our twisted thinking, which needs to get untwisted!

We have fun at Twisted Sisters. We go on camping trips to Big Sur, garage sales and service assemblies. We have gone on sober cruises, sober vacations, women's retreats and the AA International Convention. We wear badges with our home group name on it, and everyone loves to comment on them.

When you come to visit our group, we have our own meeting chips that we love to pass out. The chips are pink, and one side says, "Pink Cloud" and the other says "Twisted Sisters." Our group has a fun tradition. When we go on vacation, everyone takes a "toenails in paradise" photo—a picture of where our feet are. We have so many photos now! And we definitely seek out AA meetings wherever we go.

We always get a smile when we say our home group name. We are so lucky. We women have found a way out and a way of life that has truly rocketed us into the Fourth Dimension. Please come by and visit!

Denise R.
Santa Cruz County, California

Two old-timers, Gar and Al, are chatting after a meeting, when the thought suddenly strikes Al: "Gar, do you think there's AA in heaven?"

Gar thinks about it for a minute and replies, "I dunno, Al. But let's make a deal: If I die first, I'll come back and tell you if there's AA in heaven. And if you die first, you'll come back and tell me." Al agrees and they shake on it.

A few months later, Gar passes on, and true to his word, he comes back and finds Al at a meeting. "Gar, is that really you?" Al asks, astonished. "Yes, it is," Gar says. "So, what's the story?" Al asks. "Is there AA in heaven?"

"Well, Al, I've got good news and bad news," Gar replies. "Which do you want to hear first?" "The good news," Al replies. "Yes, there is AA in heaven," Gar reports.

"That's great!" says Al. "What news could be bad enough to ruin that?"

"You're the speaker Saturday night."

March 2003
Dave S., Ithaca, New York

Two Free Hands
September 2018

I t's a cold, dark December in Portland, Maine. I'm in an AA meeting with three months under my belt, just holding on to my seat. And here it comes, just like every other meeting this week, another AA-related announcement that starts with, "So ... NECYPAA!!!" And then like a planned call and response at a concert, a handful of members scattered throughout the room yell, "NECY what!?"

The person who stands up to make the announcement gets a huge grin on his face. "NECYPAA," he continues, "the New England Conference of Young People in AA, is going to Boston on New Year's Eve weekend to bid for the conference to come to Portland!" He goes on to explain what happens at a conference, how to get involved and how to be of service. He also says it is a way to have a lot of fun in sobriety.

Now, standing up to speak in a room of 100 strangers does not sound like fun to me, but the expression on the other members' faces, the twinkle in their eyes and the fellowship they seem to be a part of is appealing. They seem connected, with a sense of purpose. And joy. That's what I desperately need.

So with just a few months sober (which was mind-blowing and nearly inconceivable), I decided to join these "way too happy" people. Turned out they won the bid, and next year's NECYPAA conference would be here in Portland! At this point, I still didn't understand the significance of this. But I joined the host committee and stood for a position despite being obviously the newest member in the room. I was closer to a drink than others and I think that motivated me to get as far away from liquor as I could.

These YPAAs gave me a warm welcome, which was foreign to me, and I continued to show up to help plan the conference for the entire year. A whole year! I don't think I ever committed to anything for a whole year straight, besides my devoted relationship with booze. I sure as hell wasn't fond of the idea of living in Maine a year from now, let alone confident that I'd still be sober or alive. But I didn't let that discourage me; I took it one day at a time. (Funny how we start to use those slogans on the walls.) All the while, I continued to work the Steps with my sponsor.

At a shocking but still fresh six months sober, I attended my first YPAA conference in New Hampshire. By the end of that weekend, I can say I successfully socialized, laughed, danced, drank an obscene amount of coffee and made 20-plus new friends from every New England state. And I was able to do all this without any alcohol to make me feel more relaxed, talkative, fun or pretty. I now can say with all certainty that I can have fun sober.

While I was there, I had this wonderful "God moment." I ran into a newcomer I thought I recognized. I did a double take and flipped out. It was a girl I went to high school with! We immediately gave each other a big hug. I had no idea. She always seemed to have it together. Go figure.

I definitely caught the bug at this conference. I was infected with the sunlight of the spirit. In the following months, I continued to work the Steps and learned a lot about myself. I learned about my self-sabotaging character defects, how to communicate with people better and how to make amends. And through it all, this lovely, crazy, elated bunch of YPAAs have been by my side. They saw me through thick and thin and continued to love me until I could love myself. When we weren't busy every Sunday with host meetings, we were of service, went to events and showed other young AAs that you can have fun in sobriety.

I never thought I'd be dancing without a drink in my hand, but my YPAA community showed me how. And that's not the only thing they showed me I can do, now that I have two free hands. Together, we've played volleyball, spent the day at the beach, played kickball, shot pool and attended concerts. I also learned to rollerblade and chair meetings. I found out I can love myself and I can love others without needing a drink to lower my inhibitions or boost my social skills. The fun I've had this past summer has far surpassed any of my previous inebriated summers. For one thing, I can remember everything. And I no longer wake up with that terrible guilt, shame and remorse.

December came so quickly it seemed unreal. NECYPAA was just around the corner. It's absolutely astonishing that I remained sober all year. And more importantly, I was happy. Now I was that starry-eyed, loud, way-too-happy person standing up to make the NECYPAA announcements.

Our conference in Portland went off without a hitch. It was a joy seeing so many familiar faces from the local sober houses come and check out what all the fuss was about. Everyone enjoyed themselves. The weekend had phenomenal speakers, great panels and marathon meetings, fun games and music, and most importantly, it provided a safe place for 1,000 sober members of AA to come together for fellowship.

After the conference, we were still full of fire in Portland. And we wanted more. So in February, we did something I've never done before, drinking or not. We went on an epic road trip to Memphis, Tennessee to attend TCYPAA (Tennessee Conference of Young People in AA). Not only did I get to travel with my new friends across the country, but I got to experience Young People's AA with southern flair and hospitality! While there, I proudly celebrated 17 months of continuous sobriety.

Today I barely resemble the person I was just a few months ago. Each day I learn something new about myself, my fellows, the Steps and the world around me. I now believe there's no such thing as a coincidence. I call them God moments. I now live with a good friend whom I met at rehab and my sober date is the same as her birthday.

That sober fire is still burning here in Portland and our YPAA community continues to fuel it. We have now created a committee to do service work in the hope of eventually creating a Maine State Conference of Young People in AA. More new faces, as I once was, are showing up and getting involved. Most importantly, they're staying sober.

Having a good time in sobriety was not fathomable to me just a year ago, but now I can say with all certainty that what I thought was fun before, does not even compare to now. Young People's AA provided me the platform for a completely new life. What a beautiful miracle it has been.

Jenni C.
Portland, Maine

4 Continents, 1 Great Summer
January 2013

The stars aligned a couple of summers ago, and I was able to attend four Young People's AA (YPAA) conventions on four different continents, over four consecutive weekends. What an adventure!

There's an explosion of enthusiasm at YPAA conventions for recovery and living a not-glum sober life. They can be louder—and more obnoxious—than regular AA conventions. When hundreds, even thousands, of young AAs get together, the deafening roars of their collective happiness is, well, sobering. Here's a rundown of my four exciting YPAA weekends:

FIRST STOP: JAPAN
Tokyo was home for the first ever Asia Convention of Young People in AA (AZYPAA) held in July. It was a rollicking weekend I doubt anyone who was there will ever forget. And it was thoroughly put together too. The welcome packet was 32 pages long, with everything from navigating the city, food, and culture, to the schedule and highlights. It took "we beg of you to be fearless and thorough from the very start" to heart! It was also a great joy to celebrate the 35th anniversary of the first Japanese Young People's Group and to hear the person who started it. He still had the first flyer they ever made. We played at the arcade, sang karaoke and got dressed up in costumes to walk around

Tokyo. We visited shrines, rode the world's busiest subway—without losing anyone—and had an AA meeting at the top of Mt. Takao! By the end of the weekend, my sides hurt from all the laughter.

But the moment that will stay with me was when I got to hear a young woman from Japan GSO share about a thought that hit her while sitting in a YPAA convention during a moment of silence for the still suffering alcoholic. It occurred to her that over all the years she had been drinking, we had been praying for her.

NEXT STOP: AUSTRALIA

This was the second time I've attended an AusYPAA (All-Australia Young People in AA) convention, and it certainly locked it in for me as my favorite one. Great meetings and fellowship, and the spirit was, to coin a phrase—Aussie-some! There was a wonderful "Reflections by the River" meeting and the smoothest board meeting I think I've ever attended. This convention was especially exciting because the Queensland area is a part of my life in AA. When I was five years sober I moved to a remote indigenous island nearby, called Thursday Island. There was no AA there, but I stayed close to AA through AA World Service's Loners & Internationalists program. I also took two boats and a plane once a month to Cairns, Queensland to attend an AA meeting in person. I spent a good deal of time reading all the AA literature, and then leaving the books and Grapevines behind in the local Thursday Island library. After I moved to Sweden, I heard from a friend that some locals happened upon some of the literature I left in the library and began having meetings! I actually met a guy at this convention who said he has a sponsee who goes to meetings on Thursday Island, so it was great to hear they have regular meetings there now.

STOP THREE: COPENHAGEN

People were saying that this EURYPAA (All-Europe Young People in AA) was the largest AA convention ever held in Denmark. For the first time, AAs from Greenland and Romania attended and the round-the-world roll call outlasted the opening flag ceremony of the Olympics!

The meetings were really good, and there were plenty of workshops. There was also karaoke, musicians from several European cultures—and a video DJ who spun an epic set.

On Sunday morning, a friend and I crossed the bridge to Malmö, Sweden for their YPAA meeting and met a guy who was at his first AA meeting ever. He joined us that night back in Copenhagen for EU-RYPAA and told me how grateful he was to learn you could have fun and dance sober!

LAST STOP: MASSACHUSETTS

The 16th Massachusetts State Conference of Young People in AA (MSCYPAA) was held in August in Newton, a suburb of Boston. It was its second year back after a 10 year absence. The opening of the event was pumped up with live music and a sing-a-long before the main meeting. The dance was so hot the fire alarm went off! Meetings and workshops carried the message through laughter, tears and even poetry. And the closing was nothing less than inspirational, as eight people of all ages stood during the sobriety countdown for their first sober day.

There are hundreds of Young People's events and conventions held each year around the world. The granddaddy of them all is the annual ICYPAA (International Conference of Young People in AA). It's been held every year since the first one in Niagara Falls, New York in 1958. This year the 56th ICYPAA will take place in Texas, and thousands of young people from all over the world will gather together in celebration of sobriety in unity, service and recovery.

I have since gotten to serve as the Young People's contact for the Continental European Region of AA. I feel extremely blessed to have had this opportunity and to share with you about my four exciting weekends. I'm happy that young people in AA from all over the world are carrying the message to those who want to stop drinking.

In YPAA, focus is often placed on people who got sober at age 30 or younger, but that needn't keep anyone from taking part in YPAA. The AA solution works at any age. Please come join in the joy and laughter of the YPAA Fellowship. As our Big Book reminds us, "Why shouldn't we laugh? We have recovered, and have been given the power to help others."

J.G.
Stockholm, Sweden

Where the Party Is
August 2008

When people ask me these days, "How are you?" my stock answer is, "Never better." I say that because it's true. Regardless of any physical ailment or mental stress, I have never had it so good just embracing an attitude of gratitude because I no longer have to drink alcohol.

There is no entertainment comparable to a jolly AA meeting. No television, no movie, no live theater will leave you walking out the door with the feeling of joy and well-being that a good meeting brings. Where else can a person go and laugh her sides off as people share about terrible things they did while drunk, or how they embarrassed themselves, or how they fell overboard in a canoe and lost their diamond watch but saved their bottle of beer. We sit there listening and we not only relate, but empathize. And we laugh. Sometimes until tears roll down our cheeks and our stomachs ache. In all my years in the program, I've never been in a bad meeting of AA. True, some are better than others, but if we leave the meeting and stay sober another day, that will be enough.

Speaking of "that will be enough," I love what Meister Eckhart, the Christian mystic, said: "If the only prayer you ever pray is a 'thank you,' that will be enough."

A young friend of mine with many years of sobriety says this about meetings: "Hey, this is where the party is."

I agree. It's a party where a person can find sobriety, health, laughter to heal the soul, and the tools to pass on to another alcoholic on the well-paved path to recovery. If it sounds like I'm up on a soapbox or a rooftop to shout the good news of what Alcoholics Anonymous can do for a drunk, then so be it.

You can't beat it for fun. I have had more fun since I joined AA than I ever did slouched on a bar stool—or sliding off one, for that matter. "Keep coming back," we shout to the newcomer. Good idea. I will.

Dossie P.
Aptos, California

You Don't Have to Be a Hermit
September 1948

When I came into AA about four years ago I fully believed that I was committing myself to a hermitage in which I would be cut off from all normal activities and those of my old friends who did any drinking.

Since then I have discovered that many others had the same fear when they joined AA, so it's a reasonable assumption that newcomers today are steeling themselves to the same prospects.

This is an understandable fear. During the drinking years, the alcoholic tends to relate more and more of his life to liquor and to make it the hub of his activities and even his thinking. Gradually at first and then rapidly.

Then, when he has come to the realization that he can no longer control his drinking and that, in fact, he cannot by himself even stop it, he has great difficulty visualizing anything but a dreary life without liquor. Since the drinking has become an integral part of his life, he cannot see how much will be left if that is removed.

In my case, I became resigned to the idea that I needed help and that I needed AA. But I was not happy about it by any means. I joined AA with great reluctance. Only the desperate straits I had reached compelled me to go through with it.

AA's had tried to reassure me that I would not really give up anything worthwhile, and they seemed very happy in their new lives. I went to meetings and saw and heard people laughing, chatting gaily and apparently lighthearted.

But I refused to believe it. I thought they must be whistling in the dark, putting up a bold front. I admired them for their efforts to make the most of a bad situation.

Now, of course, I have learned that I was completely wrong. They weren't pretending. They really were happy.

Neither am I pretending. I'm happy and I have found that I can do anything I ever did before AA, and do it better—and remember it the next morning.

The word I would like to pass on to newcomers is that you don't have to be a hermit to stay sober. You don't have to cut yourself off from fun and friends and normal activities when you stop drinking. Sobriety does not isolate anyone. Please believe us, you newcomers. Sobriety and AA open the door to more genuine pleasure, more real friends, more interesting activities and infinitely more satisfaction than you have ever known before. In fact, it's virtually impossible to be a hermit in AA—and stay in AA or stay sober.

D.Y.

It's Not My Show
March 2021

A wonderfully talented woman I know from San Francisco, Jackie B., has been writing, directing and producing plays about AA history for a decade now. She asked me to join her troupe in 2018 for an excellent production about general service.

I was hesitant because I'm not an actor, and plus I had seen her show in Berkeley and was wowed by it, so I was intimidated. But she's persuasive. Joining the cast has been a highlight of my sobriety.

Besides being able to help share the rich history of AA—much of which was new to even a general service geek like me—there was another fringe benefit of joining. I felt like I was on a team. Jackie would encourage us before rehearsals to share with each other our sobriety dates, what we were excited or fearful about, or what Step we were working on.

One of our pre-show rituals gave me pause, however. We would do vocal warm-ups and then gather in a circle, join hands and recite the Third Step Prayer, but with a theatrical twist. We would all crouch low and start out almost whispering the Prayer in unison, then slowly raise our voices and our clasped hands until we were shouting it, with our hands above our heads. Plus, a cast member would be inside the circle the whole time performing an interpretive dance to it.

After the first time we did it, I texted Jackie and told her it had made me uncomfortable and embarrassed, but not for the reason you would think. It wasn't the interpretive dance part. It was because at that time I had 25 years of sobriety in AA, but I did not have the Third Step Prayer memorized. The reason is because I don't use it—at least as it is written. I'm certainly not trying to disparage the Prayer or anyone who loves it, but the language leaves me cold. I don't talk to my Higher Power the way Shakespearean characters talk to each other. I almost never use words like "thee," "thou," and "thy" in any other context, so why would I use them when talking to the power that has helped me bloom and thrive from the ashes of my old life?

It reminded me of growing up around the Bible. I am not knocking it or anything, but I couldn't understand it. I prefer to use straight-forward, unflowery verbiage with my Higher Power. In fact the "flare prayer" that consists of three little words, "God help me," may have been the best prayer I have ever uttered.

Anticipating alkies like me, the Big Book says right after the Third Step Prayer that the wording is optional "so long as we expressed the idea, voicing it without reservation."

Jackie assured me that I could say whatever I wanted during the warm-up. But instead, I just memorized the prayer and joined in with my cast mates in our fun and spiritual bonding experience. I have learned over the years that I don't have to be terminally unique all the time.

Although I must say, when it was my turn to be in the middle, my interpretative dance was quite unique—just not in a good way!

Tony W.
Fairfield, California

Boogying Without Booze
August 2003

My name is Susan, and I'm an alcoholic. I remember the first AA convention I went to—or got dragged kicking and screaming to, by my first temporary sponsor, a man named Doug.

It was huge: 1,800 alcoholics crowded into a large theater with several levels of seating. My temp sponsor and I were in the middle level off to the side. They did this sobriety countdown thing where everyone stood, then slowly sat down, year by year, starting with the members with the longest sobriety. The group standing was getting pretty thin under a year, and I wanted to sit down. It seemed as if I was the only one standing in a quarter-mile radius. Doug insisted I remain standing. The group thinned further. The count got to 30 days; I tried to sit down again. Again Doug insisted that I remain standing. I had only 17 days. That's when I found out.

The sound from the crowd of sober drunks exploded like thunder. They stomped, they clapped, they cheered, they whooped. I thought they'd never stop. All 10 of us with less than 30 days stood, surrounded by 1,800 of our comrades, made into celebrities by their shouts, all because we had not taken a drink for 30 days or less.

The tears wouldn't stop coming. I got it: They meant it. They knew. They knew how hard it was, what a miracle it was, how absolutely unbelievable it was that we were alkies who hadn't had a drink for a number of days.

Later that night, I saw the second indication that sobriety could be fun. They held a dance—a dance, of all things. My annoying, soon-to-be-fired temporary sponsor tried to get me up out of my seat to dance. I leaned over to him and whispered, "You don't understand. I have to have at least three stiff drinks under my belt before I dance." He grinned and pointed at the people on the floor. "They haven't had any," he said simply.

I watched them. I really couldn't believe they didn't have any booze in them. The minutes and hours ticked by. There were no fights. No one got sick. They were still dancing, and what's more, they were getting louder. They were yelling and laughing and cutting up and having a blast! I asked Doug, my temporarily-OK temporary sponsor, if he was absolutely certain that they were all sober. He pointed to one guy being carried out the door by two bigger guys. "He isn't," he said. I asked him how he knew. He answered, "He sticks out like a sore thumb." But I still wouldn't go out on the floor.

About a month later, at another dreaded dance, my not-quite-yet-replaced temporary sponsor shot off at the mouth at me right before he gave up and went to the floor alone to dance. What he said to me was, "You just think you're better than all the rest of us."

Well, I couldn't let that go without a comeback, so I chased him out on the floor to argue. At which point, he boogied and told me to loosen up. I finally did, but only to prove that he was wrong about me. I found out I dance better sober. Imagine that.

Then the straw that broke this stubborn camel's back finally came. It was Valentine's Day, and my-no-longer-sponsor, but-now-good-friend Doug decided it was time to force me out into the world of fun once more. I had found a female sponsor and had begun working the Steps, but I didn't quite shake Doug's idea that he could boss me around. He informed me that he needed a "date" for the Valentine's Dance. (I say "date" because Doug is gay.) I groaned. "But it's a speaker meeting, too!" he exclaimed. I agreed and reluctantly allowed him to pick out a dress for me.

I listened hard to the speaker that night, mostly because I really wasn't in the mood to dance and wanted part of the night to

be good. The speaker blew me away. He read the Promises "back-
ward," saying, "Whenever I took a drink, I knew a new freedom and
a new happiness." Try it. It's a real trip. There wasn't one Promise
in there that booze hadn't given me. When he was done with that,
the speaker explained that he needed to know that sobriety would
give him everything booze had given him, when it was still working.
Then he read the Promises the way they were written. That's when
I became sold on sobriety. That's what I had always wanted anyway.
And now someone was saying that if I did this deal, it would give
me all that and more.

Many years have gone by since those days. I just got a 12-year chip
from my home group. It still amazes me that I'm sober. I know a freedom I have never known in my life. I not only comprehend the word
"serenity," I actually notice when it leaves. I know peace so deeply that
I can spend hours by myself without a hint of anxiety. I have seen how
my broken life and its struggles have been of real use to others. I not
only do not regret the past, I'm grateful for it. I know I am taken care
of, and I have abundance in my life. And most of all, I know that my
Higher Power is doing for me what neither booze nor I could do for
myself.

And the fun has not stopped. It's a deeper fun now. I have laughed
harder than I have ever laughed in my life. I can talk to people and
really let my hair down, something I always said I was going to do
when I went to the bar, but never managed to accomplish. I have col-
lections and hobbies, a host of friends, and what's more, this orphan
has her very own family who loves her and accepts her, warts and all.
Someday, I hope to learn the true meaning of love. It's something I'm
paying attention to right now, and I'm keeping an open mind.

To say I am reasonably happy is to mislead by understatement.
When I came into AA, I was suicidal and remained so for five years
into recovery. My AA friends meant it when they said, "Don't kill yourself before five years of sobriety. You will be killing the wrong person."
That is certainly true for me. I expect and hope to live well into my
80s, maybe longer. And I know this happiness and contentment will

stay if I keep doing the next indicated thing: Stay away from the first drink, clean house, do my best to pass on what I have, and rely on my Higher Power. After all, the best is yet to come.

Susan C.
Woodland, California

> Heard from an old-timer: "I probably only need one meeting a week, but I go every day because I don't know which one it's going to be."
>
> *September 2006*
> *Annie R., Ashland, Pennsylvania*

Bright Spot in Tokyo
September 2013

The first time I heard about Young People in AA (YPAA) conferences, I was about a week sober. I still remember the guy who described it to me. He said, "It's awesome. Thousands of young people on the streets of New Orleans—sober!" His eyes were glowing, and he looked so full of energy and pride when he said it. But I also remember the first thought that flew through my head: Party sober? That sounds so corny.

So I started going to YPAA events in my area near Florida. And when I attended my first International Conference of Young People in AA (ICYPAA) in the summer of 2007 in Los Angeles, I had the time of my life. It was everything he had said it was—and then some. I'd never been to a bigger party, drunk or sober! I went with a bunch of people from my home group and we formed great bonds. Most importantly, I learned a lesson that sustains my passion in AA to this day: I can enjoy myself sober. I can party sober. I can sing karaoke sober. I can laugh and love and live life sober. This is the message that YPAA gave me. And it's the message I want to carry to the next alcoholic who's thinking, I won't ever have a good time again if I can't get drunk.

In 2008 at 25 years old, with one and a half years sober, I moved to Tokyo. I started getting involved in AA service there, but the one thing that was lacking that I missed from my early sobriety was YPAA.

One night after my home group I was at fellowship with my friend Jon, who was visiting from South Africa. We were eating spicy Fukuoka-style ramen noodles and talking about starting a young people's event. Would it be better to start with a Tokyo YPAA? Or a Japan YPAA? Or an All-Asia YPAA? We aimed for the fourth dimension with AZYPAA (The Asia Convention of Young People in Alcoholics Anonymous).

Afterward, we wondered why we even considered going smaller.

We only had two months of planning to do it, but the result was great. More than 100 people participated in our first-ever conference in July 2012 in Tokyo, Japan. We had guests from Finland, Sweden, Malaysia, Hawaii, California, South Africa and all parts of Japan, and an enthusiastic showing from Okinawa. We sang karaoke, we climbed mountains, we had meetings while eating "SOBA" noodles on those mountains. We also engaged in "cosplay," where we dressed in fun costumes on the streets—all the way to the Sunday night meeting. Most importantly, we carried the message of AA, and we did it with a level of passion possibly unseen in Japan until that time (especially for those who saw us in our costumes!).

This year, our planning meetings are conducted almost entirely in Japanese, and the Japanese Fellowship has responded with unbridled enthusiasm to this year's AZYPAA, to be held this September in Tokyo. People in China and South Korea are getting involved, and we're featuring speakers from Japan, Canada and Singapore. A true international miracle has begun.

To see the spirit of this Fellowship take off in others as it once did for me gives me a huge sense of hope and purpose. It's the bright spot of my life right now.

Rich H.
Tokyo, Japan

The Happy Campers
May 2013

I n 2008, my AA friends and I were taking a road trip to a St. Patty's Day supper and speaker meeting in southwestern Nebraska. All four of us had under three years of sobriety. I had heard of an old Boy Scout camp, which had been converted into an archeological and Native American educational center with a campground and two cabins for rent. The camp was on the way to where the event was being held, just a four-mile drive off the main highway. I asked my copilots if they wanted to check it out and all agreed.

The main house sat on top of a hill overlooking a beautiful canyon. Down a steep hill, nestled in a canyon depression, were the two cabins. We asked for permission, and walked down to the cabins to find them nicely decorated and furnished; the cabins used to be the scoutmasters'. An old swimming pool between the cabins had been converted into a rock garden, the deepest part of which had been converted into a fire pit. Benches made of cottonwood trees surrounded the pit.

We also found plenty of spots for pitching tents, and the area offered nice hiking trails. A small lake was located about a mile away, complete with canoes. We felt the presence of a power greater than ourselves on this beautiful spring day. We were definitely in God's cathedral. We took some photos, and a plan was hatched for a camping trip. We showed the pictures and explained the beauty of the place to a couple of other members we met at the St. Patty's Day event; they were all for it. Unknown to us, it was on this day the Happy Camper group was born.

On Memorial Day weekend 2008, a group of about 15 that included adults and a few kids returned to the camp for the weekend. We were a mixed group; a few sober under a year, no one with over five years. Ages varied from early 20s to mid-40s. In planning the trip we figured out meals and what we wanted to do recovery-wise. I am more of a grizzly camper type and had a good laugh the first morning when the battery-operated blender was brought out to make smoothies. The smoothies were a big hit, by the way. I stubbornly stuck to my campstove coffee. We had morning AA meetings, meetings after supper, and wonderfully spiritual late-night bonfire meetings. Some of us didn't know each other very well prior to the campout, but we became friends fairly fast. We spent the weekend getting closer to the God of our own understanding. Living the Steps was an unspoken theme for the weekend. The people newer in recovery got to see firsthand how we not only talked the talk, but walked the walk.

The Happy Campers' next outing was the first ever Sober Float Day. Sober Float was set up by District 14, one the largest AA districts in Nebraska, in Valentine, a town located in northwestern Nebraska. The beautiful Niobrara River runs north of town, and it hosts many outfitters who offer camping, tubing, canoeing and kayaking. The DCM for the district, who works for one of the outfitters, arranged special rates for AA members. He also set up a place for a noon cookout, meetings and a bonfire. Ex-drunks still love bonfires, especially because now we don't fall into them! Many of the same people who went camping on Memorial Day drove three and a half hours to Valentine to participate in Sober Float. We also had some new people come along for the adventure. This was definitely an adventure: I'd left the map at home, and got lost on narrow valley roads trying to find the campground. The cabin we rented was a tiny shack compared to the nice cabins we had at the old Boy Scout camp. A wicked thunderstorm the night of the big campfire meeting ended the meeting abruptly, and people had to cram into the tiny cabin or sleep in the middle of their tents to stay warm and dry.

Floating, canoeing or kayaking down the river was a spiritual experience, and wonderful beyond words. Watching all the drunk people on the river, we had plenty of reminders of what we used to be like. Once again, even with a lot of challenges, the spirit of recovery was working. We still laugh about this weekend. For those of us with open minds and hearts, we felt our Higher Power at work all around us once again.

We had a couple more campouts the summer of 2008; we even had T-shirts made that said "Happy Campers." Last year we had a banner made to identify our campsite more easily for new people. Since 2008, we have had a few campouts each summer. We always select the same camping area: a place secluded enough for open and honest sharing around a bonfire, a place where people can get in touch with their God. There is always plenty of food. People bring what they can afford to bring; s'mores and hot dogs for roasting over the fire are a dietary must. No one lacks someone to talk to if they feel the need; it seems it's easier for some to share in nature. The members of the Happy Campers are some of my closest friends. We aren't just summer friends; we are year-round friends, friends during sunshine and storms.

Sober Float has been a success and most of us have returned every year. Three years ago we made a huge canopy to ensure there was a place for meetings and fellowship in case one of those intense Nebraska thunderstorms rolled in. Additionally, it gives us plenty of shade for eating meals. If anyone is up for a good road trip, a spiritual three to seven hours floating down the peaceful Niobrara river, spending time with people who live the Steps, not just work them, then come join us.

I am happy to say we have fun carrying the message. We talk about the Steps during our meetings and during our one-on-one conversations. If someone is struggling, we suggest sponsorship and working the Steps. We have shown people how to meditate in the simplest way. We talk a lot about spirituality because what better place for Third and Eleventh Step connections than in nature? I don't believe in the Judeo-Christian God, but out in nature, I know there is a divine artist at work. I see, feel, hear and smell its presence all around me. No one in our group is overly religious, but we are very spiritual in our own ways, and this we pass on to anyone who spends the weekend with us. We laugh a lot, we cry if we need to, we share from the heart and we love each other deeply. And we don't pick up the first drink.

Scott W.
Kearney, Nebraska

Young, Sober and Free
September 2021

It was October 28, 1988, my 21st birthday. I was at an AA Halloween dance in Nashville, Tennessee. And I was sober. It was my very first time at a dance without the aid of a drink and I was paralyzed with fear. I just wanted to fit in and have fun, but I didn't have a clue how to do so without being drunk.

Out of the blue, a hippy-dippy type with two years of sobriety danced by me and suggested I pretend to be a snowflake. I felt so relieved that anyone talked to me that I just did it. It was amazing. We twirled around the dance floor and, to my surprise, we actually started a "conga line" with everyone dancing just like us. A Bon Jovi tune played in the background. We danced in our socks, sliding across the floor. It was so much fun. For a while, I was released from the bondage of self by the mere presence of a bunch of sober teenagers not giving a flip how silly we looked out there on the floor. I kept thinking to myself, I can do this!

I had intended to go to the liquor store that night in honor of my birthday. I didn't want to drink, but for some reason I wanted to buy alcohol legally for the first time in my life. I told some of the members I was with at the dance about my plans and I showed them my fake ID. They would have none of that. They suggested I hand over my ID. Reluctantly, I did as they suggested because I wanted to fit in and have friends. This time peer pressure was working in my favor for a change. What I didn't know was that by taking the action of handing my most prized possession over to the care of another alcoholic, I was taking action in my own recovery.

My sobriety was so delicate in the beginning. I remember when I got 90 days sober, I took a cigarette and burned my leg three times because I felt so numb. I couldn't feel anything. I figured that if all I could feel was pain, then I was going to at least control that feeling.

It was a difficult time. My car didn't have properly working brakes, so I would hitchhike to meetings. One night a man picked me up in his car and forced a kiss on me. I didn't have enough self-esteem and self-worth to acknowledge how much danger I was in. I just knew I needed a meeting, and the only way I could get there was to put my thumb out and take my chances. This was before everyone had a cell phone and my home phone had been cut off due to nonpayment. Slowly, I began making friends in AA and they began to pick me up and take me to meetings.

My first year of sobriety was a train wreck. I lost my car in a parking garage for a couple of months because I couldn't remember where I had parked it. A guy from AA who had a bit more sobriety than I had heard about my problem. He volunteered to drive through every parking garage in downtown Nashville until we finally found it. My car had been broken into and a homeless person was living in it. It cost me $80 to get it out of the garage and the brakes were not working well.

All this happened while I was stone cold sober. My thinking wasn't very clear in the beginning. So trust me when I say that if I can remain sober, so can you.

My early Step work consisted of the "one-two-three shuffle." Much like the snowflake dance, I twirled and whirled around those first three Steps without really committing to doing a Fourth Step. Inventorying my life wasn't something I could do at that time.

It was the other young people who held me together. They picked me up, took me to meetings and introduced me to the "meeting after the meeting." We went to AA conventions and roamed the halls without having hotel rooms to stay in. We were young, wild and free.

When I think back to some of the great ideas we had and what we thought was real sobriety, I have to scratch my head. The main thing I learned in that time of my life was that life after alcohol existed. I stayed away from the toxic people in my life who drank like I had and embraced people who, like me, had put down the bottle and learned to dance like snowflakes.

Early sobriety is hard no matter someone's age. I am 52 now and just celebrated 32 years of sobriety. I have worked the Steps and worked with others, showing them my experience. I share my strength and give hope to people who are just like me.

I smile when I see a group of young people disturbing a meeting with their whispers, crosstalk and inappropriate giggles. Those kids are the reason I made the decision to stay in these rooms. They are my people. They helped me stay sober and build a life worth living.

Valerie T.
Vista, California

1st AA: "I didn't appreciate what you said about me in yesterday's meeting, when you said a lot of us in AA are narcissistic."

2nd AA: "I was talking about me, because when I share it's always about me."

1st AA: "I know you were talking about me; you were looking right at me when you said it!"

2nd AA: "Oh, were you at the meeting?"

February 2011
Sheila R., Fort Worth, Texas

Best Deviled Eggs in Memphis
May 2013

n 2002, I was in an alcohol treatment program in Memphis. Daily attendance was required from about 8 A.M. to 4 P.M., and a half-day on Saturday. Another requirement was attending AA meetings once a day and twice on Sunday.

I began attending the ABC Group near my home. At first I arrived as the meeting was about to start and left immediately after the meeting ended. It went on like this through the five weeks of treatment and for a couple of months after. ABC Group had monthly birthday celebrations and also hosted a monthly potluck dinner. I did not attend either. After a few months, I realized this was not going to work and resolved to become more involved. I began arriving early for meetings and got to know a few people. For the birthday and potluck dinners, I began preparing a pasta salad to which I added jalapeño peppers—few people ate it. So I began preparing deviled eggs, which are always welcome. Over time I learned a lot about deviled eggs. For instance, eggs peel easier after boiling if they are a week or so old. And placing the egg carton on its side for 24 hours before boiling will allow the yolk to "center."

After about five years, the ABC Group meeting space closed. It was sad for me, but I had enough sobriety to understand that one group is not AA. I started looking for another home group, attending various meetings around North Memphis. A friend was involved with a group called On Awakening that met on Saturday and Sunday mornings at 8 A.M., so I began attending it. Our meeting space had a kitchen. Another meeting attendee, Mike T., would sometimes bring his waffle iron and make waffles, sausages and eggs. When he couldn't do it, I began making scrambled eggs. It became my routine to get up on Saturday and Sunday mornings, stop by the grocery for eggs and sweet rolls, and then cook breakfast.

After a couple of years an issue with the meetinghouse led to no more use of the kitchen. So I went to the internet for a recipe for an egg casserole. I would prepare the casserole the night before, place it in the fridge to chill, and put it in the oven when I got up. After coffee and a shower, the casserole was ready. I got a special plastic dish and cover for transporting the food. I was only preparing the casserole on Saturday; another AA member, Jo S., began making a casserole for Sunday. She already had a plastic dish and cover.

But I felt the need to go to more AA meetings than just on Saturdays and Sundays, so I also began attending a group called TGIS, for Thank God I'm Sober. They have welcomed my deviled eggs.

Recently another issue with the meetinghouse arose and our morning meeting dissolved. Most of us began attending Central Group's new weekend morning meeting, and several of us joined Central Group. We don't have a stove yet but expect to get one soon. Until it arrives, Jo and I will continue bringing our covered dishes.

For the past several months I have been preparing deviled eggs for the TGIS Birthday meeting. I am now placing a slice of black olive on top of each egg. I've also begun to prepare dinner for the Central Group Birthday meeting.

This past July marked 10 years of making eggs. My deviled eggs are sometimes referred to as "sobriety eggs." I have made thousands. And they've certainly helped me to stay sober.

Clark K.
Memphis, Tennessee

CHAPTER TWO

Creative Dreams Come Alive

Painting, singing, dancing and more—life gets busy
when we put down the bottle

During our drinking days, our talents were often put on hold—it's hard, after all, to paint a beautiful picture while hungover or to create music when falling-down drunk.

Without alcohol in their lives, many AAs experience the great satisfaction of rediscovering gifts they had never allowed to flower. As her children were growing up, Bernice S. told herself over and over that she would love to spend time cooking with them, as her own mother did with her in their tiny Nebraska town. "That dream was washed away by alcohol," she writes in her story "Faith and Flour," but sobriety makes it come true in the joy of baking holiday cookies with her grandchildren. The essential ingredients? "Flour, eggs, sugar, faith, hope and love!"

Dancing—cutting a rug, tripping the light fantastic, strutting your stuff—is something most alcoholics think they can do only when well-lubricated. Thus, the greatest fun in sobriety for many is when they discover that they can dance with the best of them, without a drop of alcohol in their systems. The anonymous author of "Dancing Machine" relates the sheer energy and pleasure he found in dancing sober at his daughter's wedding. Bambi S. gave up the dancing she loved during her years of drinking, as she found herself falling further and further into isolation, with the "music gone out of [my] life." In her story "The Girl in the Mirror," the music comes back. Sober dancing, she writes, gives her a "great rush of joy in knowing that I have been given a second chance in life."

During her first year of sobriety, Wendy D. became a painter. "Color My World" beautifully describes the hues of her sobriety: "cobalt blue, fire engine red, apple green." Painting only for her own satis-faction—"one of the first times I had done something for fun"—she has nonetheless become a professional who sells one painting after another. When asked where she studies art, her heart replies, "The school of AA." "Crayons Are My Hobby" tells the story of E.C.L., a newly sober New York alcoholic who picks up crayons and drawing paper as a kind of therapy when feeling restless and close to a drink. Sitting down at the apartment window one night, E.C.L. becomes completely absorbed in rendering the wonder of Manhattan at night. The drink is forgotten.

The old trope has it that artists have to be miserable to create. Not so with AAs. Whether they are nervously playing guitar in front of a small crowd at an AA meeting fundraiser or woodworking pine and cedar into handsome tables and chairs, the sheer joy of rediscover-ing their passion, or finding it for the first time, means "my disease doesn't define me" anymore, as Brian S. says in "A Smooth Finish."

Dancing Machine
April 2015

When I was sobering up and finally took my recovery seriously, I hung tight with AA people. Most everyone I knew was in taverns or were people I worked with. I thought everyone drank the same as me, but when I quit I began to notice that most people at work didn't drink. I had always been the instigator.

When I was still new in AA my daughter decided to get married, and being the father of the bride, I knew I'd be paying for the wedding, which was not a problem. When we made the guest list, I decided I wanted to have my sponsor and some AA people there, so we arranged for an "AA table."

At the reception, there was an open bar, the meal was great, the band came in and the party began. I decided I was going to have fun—and I did. I took the hand of any lady in the place and just started to dance. I danced to any type of music, fast, slow, whatever. I went around the room greeting people all night. I kept going back to the AA table for my tonic and lime. Some people thought I might be drinking and would get close up to smell my breath. Once, while dancing with one of the gals, she did the same thing. Finally even my sponsor asked if I had been drinking! I don't know what would make him think or ask that. I had my tuxedo jacket off, my shirt and tie off, and my undershirt had a tuxedo print stenciled on the front. All night, I'd go back to the AA table from the dance floor and tell everyone, "I'm paying for this party, and I'm gonna have fun!" I'd yell, "Let's dance," and the whole crew would get up and join me on the dance floor. They even did the bunny hop. We laughed a lot.

That night I discovered you don't have to drink alcohol to have fun. You just have to make your mind up to do it. That was over 17 years ago, and I'm still having fun without booze.

Anonymous

Crayons Are My Hobby
February 1949

This morning I got a thrill from these words in a Christmas thank-you letter from a friend: "You s-m-a-r-t thing! I love my barn. How did you find your talent?" No, I didn't build her a barn for her farm, but had the unmitigated nerve to send her for a Christmas present a framed picture of a red cow barn cuddled among the trees on a Connecticut hillside—a picture I had created in pastels, copying from an original watercolor my friend had admired.

How did I find my "talent"? I really haven't any talent, but I do have a lot of fun creating in colors on paper, although I don't know the first thing about art, and nothing about techniques of drawing or painting. In fact, I never could draw a straight line, and withdrew on several occasions from art classes in which I had enrolled in abortive attempts to try to learn how to put on paper what appealed to my eyes. It was hopeless, I just couldn't draw and it was no use wasting my time. So when I came into AA in a desperately despondent mood, and was generally jittery, unhappy and lonely, and old-time AAs suggested I could give myself a lift by buying a 50-cent box of paints and dabbling in water colors, I rolled my eyes in horror and shrieked, "Not me. I can't draw a straight line, and trying to paint would only add frustration to depression and definitely would drive me to drink. I'm unhappy, but I'm sober and just can't paint." They argued with me to no avail.

However, after I'd been dry about four or five months, suddenly one night without warning or urging, I did my first picture. I had learned that you don't have to draw a straight line in order to paint pictures, and I learned it in a rather roundabout way. I had been doing some stenographic work for an art publicist, and in taking dictation for a news release about a painter of modern imaginative pictures, the light dawned. Certainly these pictures bore little if any resemblance to reality, and certainly there were no straight lines, or, seemingly, any bother about "composition," "perspective," and other irksome (to me) details of creating a picture. Well, I thought to myself, if this woman can be a famous artist smudging a lot of colors around at will, maybe I could do it too, just for fun. But of course I didn't know how, and spurned any idea of another attempt at art lessons.

Nonetheless, the idea must have stuck in the back of my mind, for the next day on my lunch hour while prowling through dear old Woolworth's, I spied a large stack marked "Drawing Paper—25." Why not? So I bought it and fudged around the counters until I found some crayons in nice bright colors for 10 cents, and thought I'd take 'em home and maybe someday do something.

That evening at home I spent a miserable hour and a half turning my effects upside down and inside out looking for a mislaid fountain pen (and not finding it). A boresome task and I was tired, frustrated and all-rubbed-the-wrong-way—one of those times when it would be so soothing to sit down and have a good drink! And don't think I didn't think of that—because I did. But something made me think of the crayons and paper and I sat down at my window that happily affords a glorious view of the Empire State Building, which glistens and sparkles like a mammoth Christmas tree at night, and started smearing black crayon all over the white paper, then splashing it with spots and splurges of yellow and orange. I became completely absorbed in trying to put down my impression of the glow and glitter of the lights of the city at night, without worrying about form or perspective, or lost fountain pens or anything. An hour passed like a few minutes, and to my utter amazement, I had what was to me an exciting impression on paper of the night scene that gives me so much pleasure to look at night after night. True, it was crude and far from a work of art, but I liked it—and it was fun to do. And I felt completely relaxed and rested, even a little elated—and only an hour before I had been in that dangerous and uncomfortable gosh-how-I'd-like-a-drink mood. Don't know what amazed me most, the fact I had actually made a picture that resembled something, or the fact that I was so refreshed and relaxed. Anyway it's great fun, and I heartily recommend it as an interesting, inexpensive hobby.

E.C.L.
New York, New York

A Smooth Finish
April 2021

When I was drinking, I was the opposite of ambitious. On paper, my professional life was fine, but my career had plateaued. I also had largely stopped communicating with most friends and family. Regret and drinking were my hobbies, and I was good at both. Soon my life was hollowed out with rot.

Then I found AA and got sober. When I'd been home a few days from rehab, I began looking for things to do. First I decided to make, rather than buy, a storage box for the backyard bric-a-brac I had accumulated. For tools I had an old drill, a new circular saw and a penchant for mistakes.

No, plywood cannot be easily butt-jointed with only screws, I learned. Even the most earnest carpenter can build a box that falls apart. But I kept at it. I added an abundance of metal brackets to keep the box together. I added some glue, many nails and a gallon of paint and I soon had built a perfectly serviceable outdoor storage box for myself.

Then I noticed my cheap, metal patio table was, well, a cheap, metal patio table. So I learned to cut lap-joints with my circular saw and soon the crevices between the flagstones in my backyard were golden with sawdust. A lumbering but handsome pine picnic table came into existence.

I didn't stop there. Some cedar two-by-fours at the big box store became a better-than-average Adirondack chair that sat near my storage box and my picnic table. What normal people do, alcoholics overdo.

The department store bookshelves from my first apartment needed updating, so I made a set of utilitarian but stylish pine built-ins. The dining room was freshened with some simple wainscoting. That cedar lumber also became a powder room vanity countertop and a very rough looking console table. A built-in cupboard appeared in the corner of my kitchen, complete with Shaker-style tongue-in-groove cabinet doors, thanks to my new miter saw and router table.

I needed more, so I purchased a table saw and made a work bench. And I discovered the beauty of well-seasoned hardwoods like oak, maple and cherry.

I made a quarter-sawn, white oak plant stand with hand-cut mortises. I used the same oak to make a Mission-style entryway bench that required 26 mortise-and-tenon joints. A mirror framed with maple soon appeared above it. The cedar console table was replaced by a Shaker-style piece with tapered maple legs. The new pine storage cabinet I made shone with a smooth and glassy shellack finish.

Then I found myself hand-planing a lovely cherry board to make into a side table in the style of Japanese-American woodworker, George Nakashima, with yin-and-yang curves.

I was into it, whatever it was, like always. Eight months sober, but the alcoholic brain was still thirsty.

Now, an addiction to woodworking is a fine addiction to have, such as it is. Beats drinking. And I don't think it's an accident for an alcoholic to become powerless over a beautifully figured piece of walnut.

In the books by master American woodworkers of the 20th century, AA people will find familiar themes like honesty, humility, willingness, spirituality and productivity. These makers were workers among workers, keeping their side of the shop clean and finding serenity through their rough-sawn lumber and sharpened steel.

A piece of knotty pine can become the best version of itself when the laborer stays true, does not let fear overwhelm him and fixes the inevitable human mistakes with a sincere amends. In a woodshop, you'll find the friendliest, most helpful people in the world outside of an AA meeting. Nakashima entitled his memoir, no kidding, *The Soul of a Tree*. I imagine you can say the same for other crafts, like cooking, knitting or the visual arts.

Sam Maloof, another master whose furniture was beloved by American presidents and the finest museums, could have called himself an artist or designer (he was both). But until the day that he died his business card read, "woodworker."

"I like the word," Maloof said. "It's an honest word."

I'm glad there is no cure for alcoholism and, though my disease doesn't define me, I'm happy to be called one because it is an honest word. And like that new walnut chair I've been itching to make, it helps keep me sober and soulful.

Brian S.
Alexandria, Virginia

Let the Music Play
May 2013

I f someone had told me before I stopped drinking that sobriety would be fun, I would've definitely stopped hanging out with them. Alcohol was a God-given, rock 'n' roll rite of passage, and to have fun was to drink to oblivion like my heroes. I was a rebel. But with 15 years sober, it's clear to me that I have much more fun now and create more music and excitement than when I was drunk and partying all the time.

I was raised in Atlanta, Georgia and I grew up loving music. Rock was king, but I started DJing in the local clubs because disco and new wave had arrived. It was new and exciting. As a DJ, I always had access to free drinks, which became a problem fast. I loved getting totally wasted. It made me feel social and relaxed around people. But I drank myself to a point where I thought I had ulcers, so I quit for a while and things improved. But I knew that as soon as I could drink again, I would. Things improved a lot without alcohol, so I started a band and moved to New York City.

New York certainly moved my music career to the next level—and fast. I soon had a huge dance hit, making money like never before. I also decided it was OK to start drinking again. I had hundreds of people dancing to my music and coming to my parties, but now my drinking got heavier and heavier. I was partying hard every night. Soon my skills began to deteriorate. I was a mess. My songwriting came second to my late nights, and my inability to make the right career choices left me with less and less work. I became trapped in a downward spiral that led to depression and feelings that I had lost the chance to use my musical gifts. Things got really dark.

Somehow in my haze, I was able to call a good friend of mine, a former bandmate who had gone to AA the previous year. He used to party just like I did. I told him I needed help. He was happy I called. He took me to a bunch of "downtown" meetings. And I stayed. I saw that my friend was determined to stay sober, so I was determined too.

Early sobriety was really tough, but exciting. I learned to listen for the "winners"—people who had lives I admired and who had that joy of living I once had before I was crippled by drugs and alcohol. I found an amazingly patient sponsor who listened to my story and never once made me feel judged. I found new friends who made music, designed clothes and lived the rebel's lifestyle—without the alcohol and partying. Soon I found myself trying new things, like going to art galleries and cultural happenings. I started experimenting, writing music in a whole new way.

I was 38 when I came into AA, and I thought my career in music was over. But after three years in recovery, my career exploded. I started a music festival for new artists, and it turned out to be a big hit. I began DJing again, and now I spin all over the world, making friends from Brazil to Australia. I have fun playing music again. I've even written songs that have been sung by top 10 artists.

It's funny, I often feel like a rock star with my new sober life. But

I never stop going to meetings. I've been to them everywhere I work. I also never forget how dark my life was just a few years ago. AA replenishes my spirit so I can thrive as a creative artist. It also teaches me how to give back.

You can definitely call me a grateful recovering alcoholic, because I laugh and have so much more fun now than I ever used to. Thank you AA. I got the life I always dreamed of.

Larry T.
London, England

A young woman, new to AA, played hi-fi music to occupy her mind and keep away thoughts of a drink.

One day, she phoned a record shop to inquire about a new stereo album, but dialed the wrong number and got a plumbing shop. When a man answered, she asked, "Do you have 'Eyes of Blue and a Heart That's True'?"

"No," answered the plumber. "But I've got a wife and eight kids."

"Is that a record?" she asked.

"No," he replied. "But I'd guess it's above average."

May 1981

Like Madison Square Garden

June 2016

Hotdogs, newcomers, guitars, tattoos and plenty of AA coffee. This was no ordinary talent show

You wouldn't imagine it was an AA event, the way people applauded at the end of each act—not out of politeness, but from the sheer thrill of seeing their fellow members put a guitar strap around their neck and belt out a song at our group's annual talent show and auction. People stood and whistled and yelled. It didn't matter what song or poem or comedy act it was: a heartbreaking rendition of their alcoholic bottom or the eight-minute, three-note solo Sonia played at my first talent show after she'd only taken a month of guitar lessons. She said it was Zeppelin as she curled over the guitar, staring at each finger on the fretboard. But people applauded like there was no tomorrow when she finally looked up at the audience.

After having destroyed my life for the previous 11 years, and not played my guitar in 20, I was moved by her act—not the music, but her bravery—because deep in my heart I knew if Sonia could do it, the next year I could do it too.

It wasn't a small crowd to play in front of either. More than 200 people from a variety of East Village groups attended the three-speaker meeting earlier in the afternoon, ate the free grilled hotdogs and watched their AA friends play. At first glance you might not imagine the audience being so generous with their smiles and applause. Everyone in the East Village had tattoos then, some covering their faces—skulls, barbed wire and darkness. A lot of people had barely made it into AA. You could feel that. Members showed up though, with electric guitars on their backs, wearing shades and army boots like they were playing at Madison Square Garden.

The Second Avenue Clean and Dry group had been running this

fundraiser for New York Intergroup since before I got sober. By the time I arrived, it was a well-choreographed event, kind of like a three ring circus. Between each set, as the amps and musicians changed, the auction started up. Members held up pieces of art, clothing, guitars and gift certificates to local restaurants owned by sober AAs. You'd think that would be the time everyone would go get a hotdog or smoke in the yard, but the opposite happened.

One of the most intense people I've ever seen get sober was our auctioneer. He was skinny and tall and bald. You could feel his hand around your heart as he grabbed the mic and announced, leaving barely any spaces between his words, that for "25 dollars, you can own this incredible self-portrait by Sally K.!" Then he'd stare into the audience. People raised their hands; bidding wars ignited.

It was spellbinding to experience this at five months sober, but even more surreal at 17 months sober, when I signed up to perform. It happened like everything else in AA, as if God had bigger plans for us than our own. One day at fellowship, I mentioned that I might want to play a folk song some year, and added weakly if I could possibly find some people to get a band together. Tom, a professional drummer sitting at the end of the table announced, "I'm your drummer." I cried inside. It was done. With Tom on board, it would be easy to get a bassist. I'd have a band. My whole life I'd wanted to be in a band.

The crowd went nuts as I sang the Dylan song, "I Shall Be Released," and something short I'd written about my dog. The following year, I prepared even more with a larger band, and performed two original songs that we later played in a few small local venues.

In our book *Living Sober,* it says the best way to stay sober is to get busy in AA and in a world of hobbies and activities available to us. The program is a bridge back to life. Our literature talks about the gaiety you'll find at our meetings, even over the most troubling issues. I don't think the original members could have pictured Jack, one member of our group with a long pointy beard and wild eyes, as he made it to the mic each year and played an intestine-wrenching metal grind while wearing a T-shirt of himself as a teenager in the band he'd been in then. You could feel his sheer joy, though.

Unleashing my inner bonds has been a lot about what AA has been for me—in relationships, in work, with family and in creative expression. One of the women in the tiny band I formed for my second show became my girlfriend, then my wife. Sonia, the woman who played the eight-minute three-note solo my first year, had a child too, and our girls sometimes play together. It's sometimes hard to take in all the love that's available to us when we trust in the universe and join in with the joy of life. I would have been such a different person had that group not held their yearly event.

Over time, the group became smaller and stopped hosting the Intergroup fundraiser. People with more time than me explained that it was the nature of things for groups and events to come and go. The only constant in life was change. They assured me another group would someday have an appropriate space and reignite the tradition. I believe them, but I also wanted to write about it, and spread my experience that fun events like this can help AA and new members alike. It was the event of the year in downtown AA.

I trust that someone, someday, in some AA group—who has been nearly dead for years as I was—will get a similar opportunity to stand up in front of a microphone, maybe for the first time ever, sober, with their heart beating through their chest, as they see an ocean of smiling faces looking back at them. It felt like jumping off a cliff into thin air.

Josh H.
New York, New York

An old boozer went into a pub with a dog and a cat and placed the cat on top of the piano. The dog climbed up on the piano bench and began to play, while the cat sang a number of popular tunes.

The drinkers in the pub were amazed. The barkeep rewarded the old gal with a double Scotch and exclaimed, "That's a great act! Have you thought of turning professional?"

"Oh, they're not as good as you think," the boozer confessed. "The cat is tone deaf and can't sing a note. The dog is a ventriloquist."

March 2002
Dave S., Ithaca, New York

Color My World
January 2018

I n my first year of sobriety, my life changed dramatically. The most startling change by far came in the form of paint: cobalt blue, fire engine red, apple green. These colors burst into my life. I had never done any kind of art before. Now I was staying up late every night painting. Maybe it was the coffee.

I went to a meeting every evening and came home energized. I was also working the Steps with my sponsor and this gave me much to ponder. During that aching restlessness of early sobriety, I was blessed to stumble into this new hobby.

Painting is 20 percent inspiration and 80 percent technical skill. I would find myself, for example, spending hours putting leaves on a tree. At the same time, I was memorizing the Third Step prayer.

Other times, I'd be painting and at the same time I'd be trying to work something out in my mind about my father. This was treacherous Fourth Step stuff. Then, after a while I'd just be painting.

It was one of the first times I had done something for fun. There was no other motivation for it. I began to paint for pleasure. It was not for money or recognition or as an assignment. It gave me pure creative satisfaction, which was a totally unfamiliar feeling.

At six months sober, I asked the owner of our local coffee shop if he would consider hanging my art. To my surprise, he agreed. I avoided the coffee shop for several weeks after that. It was just too strange to see my paintings in an unfamiliar setting.

"Where did you study?" the shop owner asked me once. "The school of AA," I wanted to reply. Then I sold a painting! And I sold another one.

One of the sold ones was called "The Blue Tree." I had modeled it after something I worked on steadily during my first year of sobriety. I added layer upon layer of blue. Soon I realized it was the size and shape of a woman. Still later, I realized the woman was me. I renamed the painting "Self Portrait." This renaming was sort of like the awakening that occurs while working the Steps, sometimes slowly, sometimes quickly. The realization comes: Oh. This is who I am.

For me, the Fourth Step involved similar layering, both in words and in visual art. In my painting, I used the actual notebook pages that I made when I wrote out the Step. I didn't want my kids to get ahold of that stuff, so I ripped out the pages and pasted them onto the canvas, upon which I painted a redwood tree, a close-up. I did layer after layer of color, painting over the words, until I got the right kind of red. The resulting bark looked like skin. Most of my paintings were like that: close-ups.

At one year, I was finally able to paint a tree from a distance. I painted an oak tree, a real tree that I hiked to often, one that had been struck by lightning. It had lost half of itself. The old branches lay all around it while the rest of the tree flourished. I painted it all in one sitting.

The next morning, I had a heartbreaking conversation with a

friend. We had started in AA together and now, after a relapse, he was starting over. The painting's name was, "Oak Struck by Lightning," but secretly I call it "Alcoholic in Recovery."

Wendy D.
Oakland, California

A middle-aged man visiting an art museum with his wife stood ogling a painting of a voluptuous woman dressed only in a few leaves. Finally, his wife snapped, "What are you waiting for...autumn?"

September 1994
Fargo, North Dakota

The Girl in the Mirror
March 1990

have always loved to dance. There is a line in the musical "A Chorus Line" that explains my feelings about it: "All I ever wanted was the music and the mirror, and the chance to dance." When I was drinking, dancing provided me with a means of escape—a chance to forget who I was, what was happening to me, and the nightmare going on inside of my mind. Once the "buzz" kicked in—you know that feeling that comes when liquor first rushes to your head—I would make my way to the dance floor, believing that all was well. The music would begin (the louder the better), and I would be into the short-lived fantasy. My body would begin to move in a frenzy (the wilder the better), and I would believe I was someone else, living someone else's life, possessing someone else's mind and body. My new, brief identity would be that of a famous Broadway actress, a Bob Fosse dancer, or a Pulitzer Prize-winning author. Multicolored lights would begin to flash from above, the brighter the better. When the transformation in my mind was complete, I would no longer be the girl who was flunking out of school, who was out of work, who threw up and blacked out, who hadn't called her family for over a month.

I left that girl back at the table. She had no desire to dance. She didn't want to join the fun. She sat alone with her sadness. Every now and then, I would catch a glimpse of myself in the mirrors, and I was impressed. In all my grandiosity and self-centeredness, I would believe that the mirrors were reflecting a wonderful creature. Every man in the room had just fallen in love with her. When the music stopped, I would make a mad dash back to the table. I always left the dance floor with my head down. I was afraid to look up and see the illusion smashed, to realize that I was the grief-stricken girl I had tried to leave back at the table. She was always there waiting for me, staring at me, offering me another drink.

My drinking progressed. The noise inside of my mind could not be drowned out by the loud music. The voices inside my brain were deafening, and they would not stop. The flashing lights began to startle and frighten my liquor-and-drug-sensitive eyes. I would now get up on the dance floor and my legs would twist and buckle under me. Coming to for a minute, I wouldn't know where I was. Saliva would be running down the side of my mouth, and my clothes would be wrinkled. I would look into the mirror and see the grief-stricken girl. She no longer sat at the table waiting for me to return. She was now on the dance floor with me. She wouldn't dance. She would just stare back at me with a blank hopelessness that frightened me. I would try, feebly and in vain, to make her dance, or to dance her out of my semi-consciousness. But every time I looked back at the mirror, she was there.

When all of this became too much to bear, I would sniff the poppers being passed around on the dance floor, or run to the table for a drink, or grab hold of the stranger dancing with me. Anything to make the sad girl go away. But she wouldn't dance and she wouldn't go away. The music had gone out of her life. The joy of escape could no longer be turned on.

I felt only a deadly stillness that I hope I will never forget.

When I got sober, I still clung to my drinking and drugging friends. I was convinced that it wouldn't be possible to dance sober with sober people. Drunk people didn't notice my new self-consciousness, my new fear about dancing. Sober people would, or so I thought.

I now know that I thought dancing and having fun were ways of escaping from myself. My view of having fun was distorted.

Gradually, I began to realize that I had to break away from my old friends and make new friends in the program. I sat in meetings and screeched about how it was impossible to dance sober with sober people. The old-timers smiled and nodded. They promised that it would get better.

When I was about two and a half years sober, I went to an AA area assembly in the city where I had done a lot of my partying. After the business meeting, a group of AAs were going dancing. I dared myself to go along.

I took the same terminal uniqueness I brought into AA with me to the dance, but it soon evaporated. We were in the same room where I had danced to lose myself back in my drinking days. I saw that everyone else in the group was just as nervous as I was. We were all 16 again, lined up against the walls, sweaty palms, dry mouths, loud giggles, trying to get up the nerve to ask each other to dance.

I survived the first few dances, stepping on my partners' feet, bumping into other dancers on the floor, losing the rhythm of the song being played. Another part of my life was starting over. I had to learn how to have fun as a sober adult for the first time in my life. Dancing had been an escape. Now, clean and sober, I no longer needed to escape from me.

Looking into the mirrors, I saw me, smiling! I started to cry. The grief-stricken girl was gone. The music had come back into my life.

There was no noise going on, no nightmare in my mind. A miraculous transformation had taken place. The sunlight of the spirit danced all around me, with me, and best of all, inside of me.

Now, with four years of sobriety, I have a better idea of what dancing and fun is. In sobriety, I have danced naked under a full moon with a friend. I have danced by candlelight with a lover. I have danced in the solitude of my home.

When I dance now, I have an awareness of who and what I am and I have a feeling that everything is all right. And I have that great rush of joy in knowing that I have been given a second chance in life. That is what dancing does for me. That is what fun is today.

Bambi S.
New Orleans, Louisiana

Whatever It Takes
December 2008

The cute blond on the barstool reached out her hands for me. "Hey, Sweetie, did you find the ladies' room?" I nodded my head. As a matter of fact, I had, but this young lady had me confused with someone else.

As a recovering alcoholic of a year and a half, I inwardly smiled at inebriated ladies. Because I am a spoken word poet, I still sometimes frequent nightclubs and bars—strictly sober this time. "Oh, I'm sorry," she said, obviously embarrassed. "You are not who I thought you were. I'm afraid I've had a bit too much to drink."

"No problem," I answered pleasantly. "I certainly understand. That has happened to me."

The bartender refilled my glass with club soda and a lime. Although I had never chatted with him about my sobriety, he knew me well enough to keep those club sodas coming.

When I got sober, I was concerned that I would have to give up my stage appearances and my social life. Through the power of the Twelve Steps, I have learned how to avoid alcohol and continue the art I love. I had begun drinking because of my constant contact with nightclubs. Just a glass of wine here and there. Then more.

Four years later, I was a full-fledged alcoholic waking up with the shakes, downing 18 ounces of straight Scotch every night, and driving to work with a hangover every morning. That was just the weekdays. The weekends were far worse. Every Sunday I stayed in bed nursing a hangover.

A good party was when I vomited on the way home so I could sleep without the dizzy bed syndrome. My performances were characterized by slurring and giggling. I could no longer walk across a stage or daintily step over microphone cords.

What had started out to be fun had become a nightmare. The last year I drank, I lost part of my liver function. Through AA, I learned how to deal with life on its own terms and enjoy myself in the environment I still loved. The alcohol was not a threat to me. I knew what horror hid inside the bottle.

The young lady was now asking, "Don't you drink?"

"Not any more," I said, and tried to change the subject. I work hard to not make an issue out of my sobriety when I am out. I was at a poetry open mic with people who chose to drink—not at a meeting!

She wouldn't let it drop. "You used to drink?" she persisted.

"Yes," I said. "I learned I couldn't handle it. Have you heard this poet before?" I asked.

"When did you know you had to stop?" She was looking at me quite earnestly now, ignoring the poet on the stage. She really wanted to know. Suddenly I recognized that look she was giving me. She was asking for help.

Gently, I took her by the arm and led her to a quiet spot in the club. In a lowered voice, I told her some of my story. I asked her some of the questions from the AA World Services website. I ended by saying, "If you are asking yourself that question, the time to stop is probably now. Later, you may not be able to."

I told her to get in touch with AA and prayed with her to the clink of glasses and the beat of the music. That night on stage, I chose to do my "drunk poem," where I tell my story in spoken word verse. She watched me raptly. As I left the club, she smiled and waved. Her husband thanked me.

I learned that night that there is no perfect time to share the message. I must be available whenever and wherever my Higher Power needs me. I have wondered about that woman many times. Wherever she is, I hope she is doing well. I listen carefully to people out in public now. My reluctance to avoid preaching almost kept me from sharing a message with someone who was asking for help.

Lori T.
Grand Prairie, Texas

> **Karaoke bars combine two of the nation's greatest evils: people who shouldn't drink with people who shouldn't sing.**
>
> **February 2011**
> **Bob M., Green Valley, Arizona**

Faith and Flour
December 2014

I grew up on a small rented farm near a tiny town of 350 folks in Nebraska. There were seven of us kids, and Mom and Dad had their hands full keeping us in line and fed. They were devout Catholics, which helped keep us on a good track, for the most part. Many of my best memories are of the time we all spent in Mom's kitchen, which is where she always seemed to be. In June, you might find us picking mulberries or running out to collect the eggs. Mom used to tell us how her family grew their own wheat and ground it into flour when she was a kid. If they didn't store enough flour, or the bugs got into it, they went hungry. I watched Mom lean on her faith day after day just to get by, but I never really understood how she did it. We had so little, and yet she made us all feel so loved.

I remember thinking how I'd like to spend time cooking with my children some day, but that dream was washed away by alcohol and a less than happy marriage. I hated my children because they kept me from drinking, and they hated me; that was how we lived. I do not consider myself a recovering Catholic. I was not a good Catholic, and I hope my children have recovered from me. As much as I wanted to pass on the faith, love and skills my mom passed on to me, I remained baffled as to why I couldn't do it. After all, I had a great example. So what was wrong with me?

Even after I got sober I didn't seem to have the ability to live as my mom did, and it made me deeply sad to know I was not passing those gifts on to the next generation.

With no other solution at hand, I continued to work the Steps, attend meetings, talk to my sponsor and pray to a God I did not understand, with a faith that I did not have. My sponsor told me I could borrow her God until I found one of my own—and that's what I did.

In the meantime, I found myself cooking in the kitchen a lot more often, but this time with three little ones under my feet. The only way to keep them happy seemed to be to involve them in what I was doing, so my children learned early on that the plastic container drawer was for them to play in. They splashed water all over the kitchen learning to wash dishes, and I'm sure more eggs landed on the tile floor than in the cake mixes. Though we were poor, I was grateful it didn't matter if the flour was dumped on the carpet or the pots and pans got new dents.

We got better at cooking and when I went to AA potlucks—since I couldn't afford a meat dish—I'd often bring a cake or some cookies. When the holidays came around I didn't have money for presents, but I could usually come up with flour, eggs and sugar, so I started the tradition of baking cookies and giving them away to my family and friends. The kids and I had a wonderfully messy time stirring, baking, packaging up Christmas cookies and wrapping them up to give them away.

My marriage, unfortunately, did not survive, as my husband wanted to keep drinking. There were many lonely nights for me, and I'd find myself up late preparing meals for the week or baking cookies for the holidays. My children learned that if they were good, sometimes they could stay up with me and help me bake until they got tired enough to go to bed. I have many good memories of late nights listening to holiday music, making deviled eggs and fancy Jell-O dishes and frosting cookies.

As my sobriety progressed, my patience level improved, and so did my finances. Our cookies got fancier and the ingredients changed to include nuts, chocolate, apricots, coconut and raisins. Pretty soon we were baking dozens of cookies and staying up way too late for anyone's good.

I did not realize how much of a tradition this had become until my children had moved out. One day my middle daughter said to me, "So, Mom, when can I come over to bake the Christmas cookies?" She was pregnant but that did not deter her. And the tradition didn't change after she gave birth to my first granddaughter. That lil' tyke would just sleep contentedly, and we'd chitchat away till past midnight, while we happily baked dozens of cookies. Eventually my granddaughter got bigger and since she was always with us, she simply learned as she grew. She is now 9, my daughter is 29 and I am 55; and I've been blessed with 28 years of sobriety.

I've worked the Steps many times over and could not count the number of meetings I've been to. The service I've done in AA has made it easier to live a life of service outside of meetings, including baking cookies with my daughter and granddaughter.

Today, after my meeting, I was invited to my daughter's house because they had a surprise for me and wanted about four hours of my time to "make the gift" with me. My granddaughter was so excited! They had purchased three aprons and some fabric paints and wanted to make aprons representing the three generations of bakers we had become. How fun.

As we were working on this, we were talking about what it has meant to us, and how cool it was that this tradition of gathering and doing something together was passing on to another generation. We decided we wanted to write something on the aprons that would express this. After some thought this is what we did: My apron, being the grandma, has a fairly traditional design with mulberries on it and says, "Faith & Flour." My daughter's has a more modern design of the four seasons and says, "Hope & Eggs." My granddaughter's has a child's design with daisies and a heart-shaped cookie and says, "Love & Sugar." They are currently hanging up in her room until they dry; then we'll use them this holiday for our baking party.

Driving home afterward I was telling my current husband about what we had made and I realized how hard it is to express what it feels like to have hoped so badly for something, to have been so sure I'd never live that dream out and then to realize that I just had. When people ask him how his day is at work, he will often say with sarcasm and humor, "I'm living the dream." Today, thanks to AA and God and several generations of family that I almost lost, I'm living the dream with flour, eggs, sugar, faith, hope and love!

Bernice S.
Lincoln, Nebraska

A hungry drunk went to the back door of a restaurant and offered to work in the kitchen in exchange for a meal. "OK," said the cook. "Dice some carrots."

A little later, the chef asked, "Hey, what's taking you so long?"

"It's hard enough to cut the carrots into squares," answered the drunk, "but it takes a long time to put the dots on them."

CHAPTER THREE

Living It Up

Having sober fun at concerts, parties and social events

I t might be an ice cream social, a huge rock festival or a party with friends—but being able to have a good time in social situations while sober is one of the most gratifying discoveries people make upon coming into Alcoholics Anonymous. A common refrain, uttered with an air of wonderment: "I had so much fun, and I wasn't even drinking!"

In the story "Party Girl," newcomer Kay K. describes being invited to a gathering of AA women: "I observed what I had thought wasn't possible," she writes. "Sober people were having a good time. Fun could be had!" Over 20 years later, Kay is still celebrating, "grateful that a sober woman showed me how to party, and that sober friends showed up for me when I needed them."

There is probably nothing quite so giddy as a social outing among good AA friends. In "Out of the Gutter," J.L. of North Carolina depicts a bowling expedition put together by three social groups of AAs, featuring teams like "the Alley-coholics, the Out of the Gutter Gals and the King Pins!" Pretty silly, but the main lesson J.L. learns from throwing strikes (or not) is: "Play fair, be kind, let go of my desire to be right and allow joy to enter my life."

One of the greatest fears of newcomers to AA is that they won't be able to do the things they enjoyed doing while drinking. To some extent, this is true—hanging out at the bar with heavy-drinking friends is a recipe for a relapse. In the story "Woodstock II," J.E.M. perfectly captures his trepidation at attending the 1995 reprise of the original music festival. "Sure, the brochure had stated that 'no alcohol would be brought in or sold,'" he writes, "but I remember my old drinking days, and that would have been nothing more than a challenge." But what he discovers, along with a sober friend, is that he can avoid the excesses, listen to the music he loves and walk away with "more serenity than I came with."

Sometimes fun is far more personal than a music festival, however. In the story "Showtime," Mark J's alcoholism sets up a rift between himself and his mother that he thinks will never be healed, even after he gets sober. Finally agreeing to see a Broadway play with his mom, he is horrified when she picks "Beauty and the Beast." "I had not signed up to be the only adult male watching a play with a bunch of little girls." But then a miracle happens: He is transported, his mother is in tears, and they rediscover their love for each other. The touring company of a Broadway show gave two people back their relationship, which endured until Mark's mother's death almost 20 years later.

And that's the thing about having fun in sobriety. Good times can actually mean something.

Out of the Gutter
June 2016

I live in the Triangle area of North Carolina, which includes Raleigh, Durham and Chapel Hill. We have a growing group here of AA members, both young and old, from local clubhouses who meet to have a good time in sobriety. We're all dedicated to our meetings, we work our 12 Steps, we call our sponsors and work with others. But in addition to all that, we love to have fun. Life doesn't always have to be hard work, especially since we work so hard on our recovery.

Last year, three of our four local clubhouses got together for a sober bowling tournament. It was great. We had numerous challenges getting all our teams together, yet we did it, despite our concerns and apprehension. So many great teams showed up. They had awesome names, such as the Alley-coholics, the Out of the Gutter Gals, and the King Pins!

We bowled and laughed and played our best. I got to relearn many wonderful lessons: Play fair, be kind, let go of my desire to be right and allow joy to enter my life. We all got to use the things we learned from working our Steps.

During the tournament, we jokingly adapted the Steps to fit our bowling game. Here's what we came up with (this is just in jest, no rudeness meant, we must confess):

1. We admitted we were powerless over other people's bowling and our bowling curve—and when we mess up, our game becomes unmanageable.
2. Came to believe that a power greater than ourselves could help us relax while we bowl, which makes for more sanity.
3. Made a decision to turn our bowling game and our competitiveness over to the care of God as we understood Him.

4. Made a searching and fearless moral inventory of our bowling game attitudes and scores.

5. Admitted to God, to ourselves and to our bowling teammates the exact nature of our bowling errors...and tried not to do these wrongs again.

6. Were entirely ready to have God remove all our bowling defects.

7. Humbly asked Him to remove our bowling shortcomings.

8. Made a list of all our bowling teammates and competitors we have harmed and became willing to make amends to them all.

9. Made direct amends to our teammates and competitors, wherever possible, except when to do so would injure them (with our bowling ball) or others.

10. Continued to take personal inventory and keep accurate bowling scores and when we were wrong, promptly admitted it.

11. Sought through prayer and meditation to improve our conscious contact with God as we understood Him, praying only for knowledge of His will for us, while we bowl, and the power to carry that out.

12. Having had a spiritual awakening about bowling as the result of these Steps, we tried to carry this message to other bowlers and to practice these principles in all our affairs.

And one more thing...as our Serenity Prayer does not say...

God grant me the serenity to focus on my pins so I get a strike,
Courage not to get too upset when I get a gutter ball,
And wisdom to know that this is just game and it's all for fun.

We stay sober and live our lives one day at a time, yet we all owe it to ourselves to live life to its fullest. So if you're looking for a great activity for you and your AA friends, sober bowling is great fun, and for me, it's been a wonderful learning experience.

J. L.
Cary, North Carolina

Game On!
January 2014

Last night I faced my first social event of the season with my AA friends, and I wanted to pull the covers over my head and isolate. I had run out of excuses to chain myself to the couch, but somehow I managed to get moving and take a shower. The first shirt I tried on was uncomfortable, and I only own eight acceptable club shirts, five of which were dirty! So I settled for a pair of jeans, a black long-sleeved shirt and a pair of cute earrings—always a safe bet. My hair was tied back in its usual ponytail, and I still have no idea how to do my makeup. Would someone please teach me?

Dreading the evening before me, my thoughts raced. I am not your typical club-going girl, and I don't own a purse or a single pair of cute shoes. I didn't know what the style was that day, and chances are good I probably won't know tomorrow. I was convinced I would feel like a fish out of water. I thought I might want to drink to settle my nerves to "fit in." I rarely went to clubs in my drinking days, and I never went without a guy. Come to think of it, I'm not sure I'd ever been to a bachelorette party.

My car, bless its pea-pickin' heart, got me to the local coffeehouse to meet up with the other sober girls. As soon as I recognized a friendly face, I ordered a large non-fat cinnamon dolce latte with whipped cream. I struck up a conversation with one of them about her fabulous new motorcycle jacket. A friend loaned me $10, and another offered me a ride to the club. Someone took my hair out of its ponytail holder and did a quick and pretty makeup job. Game on!

We arrived at the club and I had the best night of my life. There were so many firsts: I danced and I sang karaoke—me! I also played a daring card game. Cocktail waitresses kept coming by offering shots, but I wasn't even tempted.

I'm keeping the rest of the details of the night on the DL, but as for me, I'm so incredibly grateful for my AA friends, my sobriety and the fact that, just for today, I get to be present.

Anonymous

Woodstock II
January 1995

The bands rocked, the fans rocked, and I rocked. The rains fell, the people got wet, and I got wet. The drugs and alcohol flowed like the rains coming down, the majority of the crowd got drunk or stoned, and I stayed sober. After over eight years of being clean and sober, I attended Woodstock II with some fear and reservations. Sure, the brochure had stated that "no alcohol would be brought in or sold," but I remember my old drinking days, and that would have been nothing more than a challenge. But having missed the first Woodstock indirectly because of my drinking, I decided I owed it to myself to go to the second.

I rocked with the opening band, observed the people, shot a lot of pictures and really enjoyed the atmosphere. Then I decided to head back to the tent for some faster film to shoot pictures of the next band. Big mistake—I got lost. I roamed over nearly every square inch of the 840-square-acre farm. After three hours of walking between tents, following crowds, and walking around mudholes, I found my tent. The other two people in our group also got lost. Once I got settled at the tent, I asked myself what I would have done if I had still been drinking. The answer was simple: I would have walked until I passed out, and then I would have been one of those people that other people stepped over, accidentally kicked, or fell on.

On Saturday, another sober traveler and I fought the crowd (and it was a hell of a crowd by then) to try to see Joe Cocker. Fortunately, he put on a concert worth fighting for. After a two-hour journey to get back to our tent, I decided I wasn't fighting the crowd again. I admitted defeat; the crowd had won. Our neighboring campers had put up a canopy, and I commandeered a lawn chair. And that's where I stayed for the rest of Woodstock.

Sitting in that chair, surrounded by nature, it was amazingly peaceful. The bands were up on stage knocking out their own particular style of rock'n'roll, and I didn't miss a note. The rest of Woodstock was walking back and forth less than 50 yards away, people were all around me talking, smoking, or drinking, and I found serenity in my little area.

Two other sober people in our group were up in the crowd jostling for good places to see their favorite bands, and they ended up front. One had to be pulled over the wall to keep from being smashed, and the other almost got smashed.

Sunday we were awakened by gospel singing, and then we heard Country Joe MacDonald doing his infamous Fish Cheer. My son and I embarked on a journey to find some postcards and t-shirts. We trudged, slid and slipped in ankle-deep mud the entire way. We walked between tents and over mud-drenched ones that looked abandoned. We avoided the mudholes that looked like they could swallow a car. It was a two-hour trip, and most people weren't even stirring yet. At around three in the afternoon, we started breaking camp. At four, we made our way toward our bus stop. After slipping and sliding to the stop, we were greeted with a huge surprise—a line one mile long. An enterprising young lady of our group bribed someone to let us cut in line, so we only had a three-hour wait. When we finally got hauled out, the line had grown to two or three miles long. I thanked God for patience. I realized that I had done it—I had made it through Woodstock II.

Not only had I managed to survive the long lines, high prices, heat, a cornucopia of alcohol, drug dealers, drug wanters, rain, more rain, crowds, wet crowds, no coffee, some really strange people, irritating people, mud people, and just too much mud, but I walked away with more serenity than I came with.

Although there will always be several favorite memories, one picture will always dominate. We were making our way back to our tent, music was blaring over two-million-amp speakers, the sun was way up and it was hot. Off to the side of one of the main passageways was a man, passed out with his gallon bottle under his arm, missing Woodstock II. I saw a couple of people stop and take his picture. And I thought, that would have been me a few years ago—travel all of that way, just to pass out and miss most of it.

Everybody enjoyed Woodstock II in their own way. I'm very grateful that I got to enjoy mine sober, and with sober friends.

J.E.M.
Louisville, Kentucky

Let the Ball Drop!
December 2012

"New Year's Eve is amateur night" is one saying I always seem to hear around the holidays. Whether it's actually true or not remains to be seen. One thing I'm certain about is it used to always be a tough time for me to stay sober. When I was first trying to get sober, I could never seem to get through one without picking up.

One New Year's Eve when I was in a halfway house, we were forced to go to a sober dance. I felt absolutely miserable until some of my friends convinced me to go out on the dance floor. I couldn't believe I was having fun sober. Even my face hurt from smiling and laughing so much. But then a crushing feeling came over me: I remembered that we were entering a new millennium (it was turning 2000), and since I'm an alcoholic full of self-centered fear, I had to be prepared in case the world ended. So I stepped outside of the dance at 11:55 P.M. and smoked a joint. I'm still not sure if anyone found out or not. But I certainly knew when I picked up my 90-day chip a few days later.

Then there was that New Year's Eve when I walked all the way across town to fulfill my AA coffee commitment. For my first 30 days, my home group had given me the Friday night coffee job. I even left the house extra early because I was determined to stay sober that day and not let my group down. I trudged my way through ice and snow for 10 city blocks. When I finally got to the meeting, I saw that the coffee was already made. My blood boiled faster and hotter than any coffeepot in the history of man. The chairperson had taken it upon himself to make the coffee. Didn't he know who I was? Didn't he know what I had just gone through to get there? I immediately copped a huge resentment. I stormed straight out of the meeting and straight to the nearest deli to get a beer. I figured AA didn't need me, or my help. Likewise, I didn't need it. I let that resentment keep me out for a number of years.

I recently celebrated four years clean and sober. I am approaching my fifth, hopefully sober, New Year's Eve. I use this time of year to reflect back on the past, to look at areas I need to work on and to see how I've grown and matured since becoming sober. Here's a look back:

I can't remember my first sober one! Go figure. I do remember staying sober every day out of sheer desperation. I was just going to meetings, nothing else. With no sponsor, no home group, no conception of God, my spiritual toolbox was pretty much empty. One thing I did have though, was willingness. I was somehow able to white-knuckle it through another day. Not something I recommend.

The second year, a guy from my home group invited me to a party at his house. I felt like it was a sympathy invite. I had celebrated a year sober, but hadn't really gotten into the Steps. I was still very quiet and shy, and still very sketchy in social situations. About 10 of us gathered together to eat and play games. We played a board game that involved a lot of bluffing and making up lies. It was the perfect game for this alcoholic. I was grateful for the nice sober night out, though a part of me still wondered, Is this as good as this sobriety thing gets?

In my third year, I got to chair a meeting at a New Year's Eve marathon meeting. My sponsor and a few guys from my home group accompanied me. It went well. I got home a little past 11 P.M. and rang in the New Year listening to music alone in my apartment. Thanks to working the Steps, the obsession to drink was removed and I was finally able to become comfortable in my own skin. I was OK with being alone, but didn't want to be—if that makes any sense. Right then and there I made the resolution that I was going to reach out and get more involved in the Fellowship.

That's exactly what I did, too. I started getting to meetings earlier and staying later after them. I took the commitment of greeter at my home group. It helped me to meet so many people. I became the intergroup representative for my home group. I started getting out of my comfort zone, exploring meetings other than the regular weekly scheduled ones I had been attending. I started picking up the phone and calling people more. I stopped saying no to AA. I put in the footwork, and God provided the results.

This past New Year's was a blast! I spent it at a sober party with 30 or more recovering alcoholics. Most of them I had just become friends with over that past year. We sat and talked, which was amazing for someone who couldn't say two words to another living soul a few years earlier. We stuffed ourselves. We watched TV and played cards all night. I even sang karaoke for the first time, and I was sober. The greatest part of the whole night had to be giving and receiving all the hugs once we watched the ball drop. The ability to love others and be loved by others is, in my opinion, one of the greatest gifts I have received from AA.

So this year, by the grace of God, will be my fifth consecutive sober New Year's Eve. I don't know what the plan is yet. I may try my luck at some real sober dancing this year. I'm not sure. The one thing I do know is that as long as I put God and AA at the forefront, no matter what day it is, I won't have to pick up the first drink.

Bill D.
Wilkes Barre, Pennsylvania

> A small child was watching her parents dress for a party. When she saw her father don his tuxedo, she warned, "Daddy, you shouldn't wear that suit."
>
> Amused, her father responded, "And why not, darling?"
>
> As if it were the most obvious answer in the world, his daughter replied, "You know it always gives you a headache the next morning!"
>
> *September 2005*
> *Richard M., Golden, Colorado*

Rock 'n' Roll Sobriety
May 1986

I was very apprehensive but decided to loosen up a bit and go to the rock concert anyway. I felt I had grown out of a lot of that loud, deafening music, but since my sister really wanted me to go I agreed. What the hell, I was still young—23 years old that is, and flexible enough to fit in with just about any group of people. I decided to make it a good time so I threw out my negative feelings and geared myself with a positive attitude. Thus was my mental state when I headed for the Riverfest on Harriet Island to rock with REO Speedwagon.

We got there early enough to get good seats, and I sat back to observe the throngs of people that filed past. Their eyes sparkled with anticipation and their faces gave evidence of the excitement they felt. Raw energy hung low like a heavy fog and mixed with the warm, damp air left over from the muggy day. Multicolored, greased-up hair, six-inch chain earrings, black leather studded outfits, and bright, bold, colorful sunglasses caught my eye. Nothing was unexpected, however. I was merely a spectator enjoying the show as my continuous grin would suggest to those passing by.

The concert was finally getting underway and my friends needed more beer, so off they trotted to battle the crowds and long lines while I attempted to save their seats. Of course they missed the first song, and almost lost their seats. While I was dancing and clapping to the music I could see them off in the distance as they jostled their way through the crowd, trying to save their sacred beer from spillage. It seemed an eternity, but everyone finally settled in.

By this time the band was working up a sweat and the crowd's intense energy was growing. It didn't take long before the familiar smell of marijuana played on my senses. Oh, God! I decided right then and there to thank God for my sobriety. It seemed only yesterday when at this same concert I was too stoned to even realize what songs were played. Hard rock is tough to figure out anyway, yet at least tonight my mind was intact and I could actually distinguish one instrument from the next and figure out the rhythm.

Unfortunately my enthusiastic, absorbed state was interrupted. "What d'ya want?" I screamed at my sister over the grating sound of heavy metal.

"We have to go to the bathroom," she yelled. I had forgotten that wretched curse of beer drinking.

"Ok," I shouted, "but hurry back. I can't be saving seats all night." Off they went again while I continued to enjoy the show. Yes, by God, I was enjoying this concert.

All around me people were losing their balance and falling off benches because of the effects of alcohol and drugs. Yet I firmly held my ground and confidently stepped up my movements in the tiny spot I inhabited. I was amazed at the amount of control I felt amid all this unleashed energy. Sweating bodies were pushed and shoved in the whirlwind of mass chaos, while endless screaming mingled in the air with pounding drums and electrifying acoustics—still, I was in control! My thoughts were soon disturbed by the scrawny kid next to me.

"Do you have an extra joint?"

"What?" I exclaimed, clearly flabbergasted. He was maybe 15 or 16.

"Do you have any extra weed, man?" he repeated, somewhat hesitant this time.

"I wouldn't even have a match to light one for you," I answered. He didn't seem to believe me, but I really couldn't help him. I looked at him again and smiled.

Half an hour passed before I saw the familiar faces of my sister and her friends. They were having trouble getting through the wild crowd. Too bad they were missing the whole show. When they finally made it, I informed her that they had played her favorite song. "Don't go to the bathroom," she shouted in my ear, uninterested in my comment. "You wouldn't believe how long the lines are."

As she continued to be preoccupied with lighting her cigarette and carefully guarding what beer she had salvaged, I absorbed myself in the excitement of the live music and the fact that I was seeing—really seeing—REO Speedwagon for the first time.

The thoughts and emotions that coursed through me that night are almost inexpressible. I recognized a year and a half of growth amid the blaring, screeching, deafening sounds of electric guitars and synthesizers, and saw for the first time that this was what self-esteem was all about. I was not afraid to do my own thing in this crowd. I was not worried about how I looked, nor intimidated by how others looked. I was not comparing myself to others; I was not crazy, and felt no need to act crazy; I was definitely not unhappy; and I was not thirsting for attention and acceptance, or trying so hard to feel that I belonged. I was not inside looking out, rather I was outside looking in.

I stood in the middle of 35,000 people and felt free to be a different, unique individual. The most important part of it all is that my Higher Power was with me and I was conscious of him. How many other people in this rowdy, rambunctious crowd were thinking of a God and feeling the greater effects of his energy and power? How many times while I was drinking did I become conscious of my Higher Power and my inner feelings? I can't think of one. The only times I remember being aware of that is when I cried out in pain and desperation. He was there then, but I couldn't see him through my tears, my darkness, my raw pain.

"Did you have a good time?" I asked my sister when it was all over.

"Yeah, it was great," she answered, but quickly changed the subject to the amount of beer that was spilled on her. I could plainly see the effects of the concert were short-lived. Tomorrow she would not remember the real music, only a loud, undistinguishable sound and a lot of people. I, however, had discovered a new dimension to my sobriety, and it was well worth a hard-earned six bucks!

B. Z.
St. Paul, Minnesota

Party Girl
October 2004

A woman at our Los Angeles area clubhouse used to say, "I didn't know I was an alcoholic; I thought I was a gourmet cook."

As a farm wife in the Midwest, I thought I was a gourmet cook too, and when AA members told me I would be giving up drinking alcohol as well as cooking with liquor, I could see that the rest of my life was going to be very boring.

With my nearly-sober brain I saw an utterly flat landscape ahead— no drinking, and also no parties and no fun. I couldn't imagine what form of faith these people had that was sustaining them and their happy smiles while having no enjoyment in life whatsoever. What could they possibly have to look forward to?

In early sobriety I stayed with my sister in southern California, and a woman at the nearby clubhouse where I was attending meetings invited me to a party at her house. "We'll be celebrating some AA birthdays and having some fun. As a newcomer, you should be there," she said. She was right. I walked into her house and the party was going on. It was all women, as I recall, happily greeting and hugging each other, laughing, eating and drinking coffee.

I was stunned. There weren't enough chairs and someone told me to sit on the floor. From that vantage point I observed what I had thought wasn't possible. Sober people were having a good time. Fun could be had! Not by me, probably, but I could see genuine happiness in these sober women.

That year the Midwest became locked in the coldest winter in 125 years, and I had to return to the business I'd left behind. I qualified at that time for low-rent housing, so I moved into a newly-constructed multi-unit building at the west end of town. At first, I was the building's only resident. My little apartment had icy-cold floors and occasionally frozen plumbing, but it was new and cute, and my sponsors were telling me it was time to start living on my own. There I read my AA books and went to the local twice-a-week meetings when weather permitted. I felt very alone.

Sober, lonely and cold in my new dwelling, I thought of the AA party I'd been to on the West Coast. I decided I could have a party! I could invite friends from my meetings over and they would warm up my new home. (That's why they call it a "housewarming"—I got it!) At that time Midwesterners didn't have the "birthday" celebrations I'd seen out West, but I knew how to put on a party and I now had some sober friends.

Of course, the party was grand. Happy to be invited, my AA guests came with their spouses and sponsees, and brought warmth and smiles to my new home. I made a hot punch of cranberry juice mixed with apple cider and served it with a soup ladle out of a slow cooker pot on my little kitchen counter. I had also stocked up on plenty of ice cubes, as I knew a good hostess should. When morning came, I remembered everything that happened and everything that was said at my party, and I had to laugh because not a single ice cube had been needed.

Sober entertaining is different from drinking days, but it is fun, and the rewards of the sober life are worthwhile in this enduring AA Fellowship. I am grateful that a sober woman showed me how to party, and that sober friends showed up for me when I needed them.

Those two parties, so important to my recovery, were over 20 years ago. I've cooked a lot of nonalcoholic party foods and been to a lot of parties since, and this year I celebrated my 22nd sober Christmas.

Kay K.
Redondo Beach, California

"We're invited to a cocktail party," a wife informed her husband.

"But I've been dry for three whole months!" he exclaimed.

"That's probably why we're invited," she said.

May 2005
Anonymous, Wichita, Kansas

Showtime
March 2021

I've seen a lot of miracles take place in recovery, and I'd like to share a personal experience that I consider to be nothing short of miraculous: An amazing transformation between a mother and son that would have never happened without AA.

To say my mother and I had a tumultuous relationship for 35 years would be a vast understatement. And me drinking heavily from the age of 13 didn't help matters. Early on, my mother and I pulled through some very hard times together. But then I lost myself. By the time I was 35, my mother and I were through with each other. She even told me never to call home again because she hated the person I had become. I told her I didn't care what she said, but deep down in my heart I really did.

While drinking, I became a victim of my own behavior. I alienated everyone I ever cared for and destroyed all my relationships with family, employers and friends. I reached a point where I was only living to drink. I knew the end for me was near if I didn't stop drinking. Somehow, I knew that I didn't want my relationship with my mother and others to end this way. After reaching incomprehensible demoralization, I came into the rooms of AA desperate for something to change.

Until I got sober, I always refused to ask for help. But in AA, I did the exact opposite and got a sponsor. They called him Make-Your-Bed Bob. What a gift he turned out to be. I truly believe the old saying that "a meeting might save your butt, but a good sponsor will save your life," because this sponsor sure saved mine.

When I first mentioned my mother to Bob, he suggested I read "Freedom From Bondage" in the back of the Big Book. My initial reaction to the story was to look for differences instead of similarities. I thought the story didn't pertain to me. Besides, I wasn't big on praying at all and I certainly didn't want to pray for people I resented. Fortunately, my heart drowned out the noise in my head and I reread the story, this time looking for similarities. Afterward, I found myself praying that my mother would get the same things I wanted in life: peace and happiness.

By the time I achieved two years of sobriety, my sponsor said it was time to make the amends that count the most, the amends to the living. That meant my mother.

In those two years, I had only seen my mother once, on neutral turf, when I made a Ninth Step verbal amends to her. Even that was difficult. A visit at Christmas three years earlier had been the last time I was at her house, and because of my drinking, I was asked to leave within the first hour of my arrival—even after traveling 1,100 miles to get there. Now, unexpectedly, she had invited me to visit her and her husband.

Sober, nervous and expecting the worst, I went to their house with a plan. Regardless of whatever my mother or stepfather did, I was going to keep my side of the street clean and not cause any more harm. Bob suggested I do something nice with her. He encouraged me in his grumpy, old-man voice to "ask her what she wants to do and do it, whether you like it or not."

Soon after I arrived, while eating lunch with my mother and step-father, I "acted my way into good thinking" and asked my mom if there was anything she'd like to do while I was there. Her blue eyes lit up and she quickly responded, "All my life I've wanted to take you to a play and there's a great performance at the theater right now. Will you go with me?"

My first thought was that she must be out of her mind. Me, go to a play? She had to be kidding. I wasn't much for the arts growing up. I had been far too busy drinking, fighting, going to jail and hating everybody and everything. But I surprised myself with my answer. "I'd love to," I said. "Let's go." At once, my mother leaped up from her seat and made calls to get tickets. My stepfather turned and looked at me with a puzzled, steely frown. "What's this all about?" he asked.

"I'd rather have needles stuck in my eyeballs than go to this play," I told him, "but I know it's important to her, so I'm going to go." The look on his face slowly changed, and for the first time it seemed like my stepfather actually respected a decision I had made.

Meanwhile, my mother made what I considered extravagant plans, which I dreaded. I thought going to jail might be easier to endure. She informed me that we would go for a nice lunch before the play and that I needed a nice coat and tie, which I didn't own. She insisted that we go shopping because she knew I'd have no clue what to buy. I knew this outing would be a major challenge for me because in the past my mother and I couldn't be together for more than five minutes without arguing.

Somehow, without going completely insane, I survived the trial of clothes shopping with my mother. At times I thought I was going to lose it, but I got "prayed up" and remembered the primary purpose of my visit was to make living amends to her. It was hard. Trust me.

The big day came and there I was, wearing dress pants, a nice tie and a new blue sport coat, eating lunch with my mother. The lunch turned out to be pretty good. I could sense that she was overjoyed; the day she so longed for with her son had finally arrived. Her good spirits actually lifted mine and there was little to no tension.

After lunch, we crossed the street and I found myself standing in line surrounded by a loud sea of little girls and their mothers. Bewildered, I asked my mother, "What the hell is this?" Responding in her traditional way, she answered, "Oh, shut up, you're going to like it. It's Beauty and The Beast and the actors are from Broadway."

While my ego initially focused on the "shut up" part, I swallowed hard and kept silent. My self-centered thoughts reminded me that I had not signed up to be the only adult male watching a play with a bunch of little girls. A self-induced hurricane roared in my head. But I kept asking my Higher Power to help me remember my primary purpose and to guide me through the day with grace and dignity.

After taking our seats in the large auditorium, I apprehensively looked around the theater filled with happy women and squealing children. I wondered why I let my sponsor talk me into this mess. After a few minutes and some deep breaths, I finally surrendered, knowing it would all be over soon.

The curtain rose and I sat back and watched. And something unexpected happened. Having never seen a play before, I became amazed at the talented actors and actresses. Something magical transpired and I became absorbed in the story. While teacups swirled around and candles danced and sang, I looked over at my mother. She was beaming with joy. I had never seen her that happy with me since I was a small child. Astonishingly, I felt happy too. It would have been hard for me to admit this back then, but when the lights came on at intermission my mother turned to me, smiling, and said, "Well, what do you think?"

I simply could not answer her. I'd been through some hard times in life and was never one to cry, but with lips trembling and tears slowly streaming from my eyes, I couldn't speak. I was overwhelmed with love, the kind of love both my mother and I always wanted and, while it may seem silly to some, for the two of us to be truly enjoying time together was nothing short of a miracle.

It was also a beginning. After that weekend, I left that coat and tie at my parents' house, and over the following 19 years, there were more plays. More importantly, I was always welcomed at their home, and I was there for both my mother and stepfather when they passed. On each transition, their final words to me were that they loved me and were proud of me. That is one of the greatest gifts I have been given and it would have never happened if not for AA.

Mark J.
Kona, Hawaii

During the wet period of my life while living in New York City, one night, well loaded, I went to see a play. At the intermission I ducked out a side door, found a bar, and poured down some more booze. Returning to the theater, I found a woman in my seat. I didn't want to cause a disturbance so I sought out an usher and explained the situation. After a brief conversation the usher said, "Your trouble, sir, is that you're in the wrong theater."

July 1985
C.J., Wisconsin

Ice Cream People
February 1979

One day at a time, AA has me off the bottle. Each day, things are much better and I have more use for my feelings. And there are even bigger changes in the nights. Instead of listening to hard rock and soul through a smeared haze of smoke and gin and beer, we face new complexities in 31 flavors: bubble gum, strawberry cheesecake, chocolate mint, rocky road, etc., etc.

We park outside the store and look at the ice cream people, a very healthy and satisfied people, nary a potential suicide in sight. These people probably even vote in the city elections! I say to you, "What if the fellows saw me go in there? Suppose they find out I'm going in for a banana boat sundae?"

"Come on, chicken!" you laugh, and we go in and stand with the ice cream people. None of them are cursing or threatening to clean out the store. There seem to be no hangovers or grievances. I am alarmed at the peace and calm that flow about me. I feel like a gorilla in a beauty contest. We finally get our sundaes and sit in the car and eat them.

I must admit they are quite good. Curious new world. All my friends tell me, "You're looking good, man. We thought you were going to die there for a while." Seemed like a long, long while—10,000 nights of drunkenness, drugs, jails, prisons, hospitals...

Later this night, we know closeness and love and we speak of easy things, lying by an open window with moonlight looking through.

The ice cream people make me feel good inside and out. Quick, give me a double shot of strawberry!

M. O.
Brooklyn, New York

> Four drunks were found nearly frozen to death in their car at a drive-in theater. One of them, after he was brought back from the brink of death, informed the doctor that they had driven in to see the movie "Closed for the Winter."
>
> *December 1978*

Unity at the Music Festival
July 2011
Online Exclusive

The First Tradition typically applies to Fellowships functioning at Alano clubs, churches and civic facilities where daily or weekly meetings are held. But it also applies to a circle of AA friends who meet twice a year under conditions that are not particularly conducive to sobriety. Here, we may be far from the madding crowd, but we are squarely in the middle of the partying crowd. The concepts of our common welfare and unity enable us to carry the message and ensure that we are carried safely and soberly back to our home groups throughout California and as far east as New York.

I'm referring to the AA Fellowship at the biannual music festivals in Yosemite, California. During four days over Memorial Day weekend, there are 3,000-plus festival-goers, and over Labor Day weekend up to 5,000 campers at this High Sierra event. Although there have been AA meetings at the festival since the 1990s, in 2006 the festival management granted the request of several AAs to establish a permanent location for our meetings in the Pines.

Our refuge, known affectionately as Camp Drink No More, is located near the middle of the 360-acre festival grounds, which are comprised of mountain meadows surrounded by towering pines. We are located up the road from Camp Stand Up No More and down the road from Camp Party Til You Drop.

Given its location along the main thoroughfare, Hog Ranch Road, Camp Drink No More is a refuge hidden behind 60 linear feet of tarps, which protects our anonymity and facilitates attraction rather than promotion. It's amusing to sit unseen behind the tarps and hear passersby snicker at the notion of not drinking at a music festival. The sign has the familiar circle-triangle symbol with "Friends of Bill W" off to one side. I overheard one lady on the other side of the tarp explain, "Oh, they're all friends of that Bill Wallace feller!"

You've heard of skating on thin ice? Well, imagine yourself, newly sober, in a sea of tie-died mamas and long-haired daddies pursuing uninhibited enjoyment of music in a campground setting. Most Camp Drink No More AAs share my story, having experienced these festivals as both sober and not-so-sober alcoholics. So when we come back newly sober, we're burdened with old party memories and faced with new party temptations. Talk about slippery places! The irony of AA's unity is that the thin ice gets thicker the more of us there are stepping out onto it in faith, holding hands and looking out for each other's common welfare. Unity and common welfare come alive when someone 30 years sober embraces someone 30 days sober.

"Keep coming back" takes on a whole new meaning when we're from all over the country and see each other only twice a year. While roaming through the masses during these four days there are hundreds of encounters with other AAs whom we've just met that morning or maybe last year. There's always a smile and a nod, the knowledge that we're not in this alone, which are expressions of unity promoting common welfare. In lieu of a secret handshake, we extend a covert wink, a nod, or a be-well hug. Several years ago, an "old drunk from Texas" produced small buttons to wear on our hats and clothing that proclaim our camp name in fuzzy, illegible letters, so that only we members can identify one another from a distance while remaining anonymous up close.

Since the last festival, two of us lost children and others lost parents or close friends, so the sharing this time was about dealing with the loss of loved ones. If old enough, every one of us has lost a close friend or family member, but not every one has the opportunity and privilege provided by AA to share our losses with imperfect strangers who sincerely care. This time, several AAs attended the memorial service for a member's daughter to extend our love and support to him and his family.

As our friend from Fresno likes to say, "If we could drink normally, we'd do it all the time!" A newcomer shares that if not for Camp Drink No More, he could not trust himself to be at the festival. Another member shares that the festival is really an AA retreat where they happen to play music. I clearly remember my first sober festival back in 2005. I had been sober three months, since Memorial Day. I had done my 90 meetings in 90 days. My home group in Wrightwood, California knew that I was anxious about my first sober festival in 28 years, so they were praying for me 375 miles away. When I came back home sober, the Wednesday night meeting erupted into cheers and applause welcoming me back! It's amazing how far and fast prayers travel in AA circles spanning an infinite number of miles!

Back then, as I walked along Hog Ranch Road sober for the first time, my attention was captured by a wooden sign depicting the familiar circle-triangle symbol and the three legacies of Alcoholics Anonymous: Recovery, Unity, and Service. My heart did a little jig and before I ever met a single member of Camp Drink No More, I knew who they were, where I belonged and that I was home!

Ed
Wrightwood, California

An older gentleman was discussing his longevity. "I have never allowed alcohol to pass my lips," he declared, "never smoked or chewed tobacco, never went to a nightclub, dance, or movie. I don't watch TV or listen to the radio, I don't drink coffee or tea, and tomorrow I'm going to celebrate my 90th birthday."

"How?" somebody asked him.

September 2006
Eric E., Scottsville, Michigan

Front Row On Fun
August 2003

Last Saturday night, I sat in the front row of a comedy club, my arm around my boyfriend, glass of ginger ale in hand, laughing hysterically. I was sober.

My boyfriend and I returned home by subway, repeating our favorite acts and cracking up all over again. There was no fighting, no desperate need for a drink and no desire to get plastered.

To the nonalcoholic, a night like this may seem normal or even average. Once upon a time, for this alcoholic, a night with laughter and hysterics, without alcohol, was unimaginable.

Since taking my last drink, I've gone to writing circles, theater events, holiday parties, amusement parks, dinner parties and sporting events, both actively playing and watching. I've participated in more social gatherings (that I remember) than all the time I was drinking. I have never had more fun in my whole life! I drank for about 10 years. I've been sober for two.

I used to think that having a pint was the only way to have fun; now I know that, for me, it's the only way to destroy the fun that I'm having!

Kate Q.
Toronto, Ontario

Bright Lights of Fun
January 2013

I have watched a few precious young people coming into our program lately. They stay sober a few weeks or months, then drink because they don't understand how they can have fun without drinking. It's just a bizarre concept to them. They get into social situations, whether by choice or necessity, and revert back almost instantly to the delusion that bright lights of fun are just beyond the next drink, when indeed the bright lights are spinning from the top of a police car.

When I was young in sobriety, having fun without drinking was inconceivable to me too. So much blind faith was required; it was just more than I could muster. But people in AA told me I could borrow their faith. They also told me that they had already gone to the detoxes, jails and hospitals for me many times and that I didn't have to go. That was a relief. I had to trust that these really "old" people in their 30s and 40s had something I wanted, even though I didn't want it yet, nor even know what it was. I can't explain why I had the precious gift of desperation as I didn't know I had that either.

Even though I was rageful and rebellious, my feet did what I was told. During those first 90 days, they told me to stay away from those people, places and things that made me feel like drinking. I took a leave of absence from my job and concentrated only on sobriety. Sobriety was like learning a new language in a foreign country. In order to survive, the first words I had to learn were, "No thank you." How could I believe that turning down one drink could improve my life geometrically when I couldn't wrangle basic arithmetic?

All I could do was believe for one hour at a time that all these people were not lying to me and that their lives had changed dramatically and mine could too. I didn't know if I was an alcoholic, as obviously I was too young. And who knew if I wanted sobriety? I only wanted that pain to stop and to just feel OK. I hadn't felt OK in my soul in a long time.

The definition of fun was different before AA. At the end of my drinking, when the puppy had become a raging lion, I was trying to have fun but couldn't find it. Was it somewhere between the fourth and fifth drink? Was it in California? Was it in Macy's? Was it in that stranger's eyes at the end of the bar? Unlearning my old definition of fun to find true joy and unlearning my religion in order to find a loving God were two of the most important track switches I had to make in my brain.

It's now 35 years later. Last week, I was on vacation with 130 fellow alcoholics, and a big group of us went to a comedy club. When the comic on the stage kept calling one of our members in the front row the "Drunken Lady," the rest of the people in the room couldn't understand why our section was howling. At the end of the performance, we crawled out of there crying from laughing so hard. No one has a lust for life more than a bunch of sober alcoholics!

The blindness of new sobriety is kind of like the white noise that used to be on the TV screen at 3:00 in the morning. We are blank on what fun is. It has to be redefined. What I truly seek now is joy, contentment and authentic belly laughs. For this alcoholic, being willing to unlearn has been as important as being willing to learn. The circle of my world was very small in the beginning, but it has gotten wider and wider over the years. There is no place now I can't go and have a good time.

My best times are still when I am with my sober brothers and sisters. Being with people who have been brought back from the dead makes every adventure we experience together so much sweeter, and the frosting on the cake is that God meets us everywhere we go!

Snow P.
Ft. Lauderdale, Florida

Two drunks were comparing their dreams. Said one: "Wow, did I have a great dream last night! I was at an amusement park and they had the most incredible rides I've ever been on. Never had so much fun in my life."

Said the second drunk: "I dreamed I was out on a date with Marilyn Monroe and Brigitte Bardot."

First drunk: "You louse—why didn't you call me?"

Second drunk: "I did, but you were out at an amusement park."

September 1962

Chapter Four

The Great & Glorious Outdoors

Hiking, swimming and horseback riding—enjoying some
fresh air and a good sober time

here's nothing like the great outdoors for sober alcoholics to
shake off the cobwebs, exercise, have fun together or sepa-
rately and find spirituality in the grandeur one can encoun-
ter. Generally speaking, this was not a part of their existence while
drinking. As Curt W. puts it in the story "Grabbing the Gold," his
paean to crabbing on Puget Sound: "I now live a life I only dreamed
of and often fantasized about from a barstool."

Life isn't all lobster sandwiches and whoopie pie—or is it? In
"Greetings From Maine," AA friends Diane S. and Carolyn H. head to
Acadia National Park to go hiking and biking. Back when they were
drinking, vacations were "an excuse to get even more wasted than
usual," but their week-long trip allows them to hike up mountains, go
whale-watching, indulge in Maine food specialties—and appreciate
not only the beauty of their surroundings, but "the beauty of unconditional friendship."

The Coffee Cup hockey tournament, described succinctly in the
story "Fellowship on Ice" as sober men playing "without beer," takes
place every year in Ontario. Author Marty C. writes that the tournament is "based on AA principles [and] has lasted for 25 years." Hockey can be a physical and fiercely competitive sport, but AA is present
in every game's Serenity Circle, where all players and even non-AA
refs get together at center ice to say the Serenity Prayer and reaffirm
"the power of AA fellowship that holds us all together."

A dream long held by Lorraine M. was to go horseback riding on
the beach. On her first sober vacation with seven other sober women,
she decides to try, even though she has never been on a horse in her

life. In her story "Let's Do This," she describes her struggle with anxiety as she mounts the horse, but the animal turns out to be "a very gentle soul" who is patient with her. "I rode my horse into the ocean," Lorraine writes. "She loved it and so did I."

As the stories in this chapter illustrate, the outdoors is a place where health, sobriety, spirituality and gratitude meet. "Fireflies, Ghost Stories and Campfire Coffee," describes a magical scene of AA fellowship among a group of transgender AAs on a camping trip. As member Lucky M. describes it, they celebrate sober birthdays, hold meditation meetings "while half-dipped in the lake on the sun-speckled rocks," and huddle around the fire singing songs and telling ghost stories. "I'm so grateful," she writes, to celebrate "a new life of love and service."

A Big Splash
January 2002

Tubing! When I was drinking, I thought this was the ultimate cooler for the dog days of summer. Lying on inner tubes, my friends and I would float for hours down the local river. The beer had its own tube, so we were never far from our liquid good times, though those good times often led to vomiting after the first stretch of white water. I couldn't wait to do it all over again.

After a few more years of this kind of drinking, I crawled into AA. A growth opportunity soon presented itself to me in the form of a tubing trip that friends from my home group were planning. I didn't want to go because I always had been drunk while tubing. I thought I'd have to sneak beer just to be able to socialize.

But my sponsor told me, "Sobriety is progressive, too." I had learned that following directions allowed the best in me to surface, even if only for a short time, when I had the courage to face a fearful event (like my Fourth Step, for example). Deep down I felt I had no courage, yet I was sober and had made it to the other side of Step Four. A quiet gratitude to God began to take root in me.

I now had the opportunity to learn from past success. If I didn't drink while doing the Fourth Step, I wouldn't have to drink on this tubing trip either. My sponsor calmed my racing mind. She told me to go tubing and have a good time. Learning to socialize was just another fearful event for me. So with grim determination and the social skills of a clam, I decided to go tubing and have a good time—if it killed me.

I was uncomfortable until I saw the friendly faces of the people in my group. I grabbed my tube and plunged into the water. I recall laughing throughout the day—a lot. There were jokes, teasing, hamburgers, hot dogs and soda. Once I entered the water, I didn't even think of my prior tubing drunks. Freedom! AA had taught me that past events could be redefined into occasions for fun. AA had taught me how to live.

Kathy R.
North Carolina

Greetings From Maine
August 2013

Hiking and biking? That was not our idea of a vacation when we were active. Back then, vacations were an excuse to get even more wasted than usual and engage in self-destructive behaviors. But living sober means finding new ways to be present, alive and in conscious contact with a Higher Power. So my friend and I decided to go on a vacation to Maine and visit Acadia National Park.

We know each other from a Monday night women's meeting. Earlier in the year we took our first trip together to an AA Young People's Conference in the Adirondacks. We got along really well and liked hiking because it felt so healthy—physically and spiritually. So we figured that going somewhere neither one of us had ever been, filled with woodland trails and coastal treks, would be a good idea. Our plan was to spend a week enjoying nature, friendship, new meetings, and let's be honest, the occasional lobster and whoopie pie.

Here we come, Maine! Two girls from the suburbs with our survival knapsacks and self-knowledge. The car was packed with too many outfits, good music and luckily, a reliable GPS system. The 10-hour drive went by rather quickly. We had hysterical conversations about how we tend to take others' inventories and, of course, what we needed to do to survive in case we got lost or were attacked by a moose. (By the way, neither of these happened.) Our accommodations were in a great location. We could walk to town and take bike rides to the park, but best of all, the three AA meetings we attended were right on our very street. Coincidence? We think not!

Our experiences so far in the rooms, and this sober adventure in particular, have helped us recognize that when we were drinking, the dynamics of a relationship weren't a consideration, never mind a priority. We didn't care about what others wanted or needed because it was all about us—planning our next drink or manipulating others to get what we wanted. Today, as a result of working the program, we're able to see that there are so many experiences to be a part of. We can now appreciate the beauty of unconditional friendship and not allow our fears to dictate what we do or who we let in.

While in Maine, we certainly had to practice patience, tolerance and boundaries. As hard as we try, there will always be things that trigger our character defects. But today we don't need to act on those triggers because the program gives us the tools to deal with life (even during vacation) on life's terms. Our ability to support each other on the steepest hills of a bike ride, take turns navigating a trail, and come to a compromise about our plans for the following day, were all gifts of our sobriety. Living a sober life means crying tears of laughter and gratitude as opposed to tears of regret and shame.

We couldn't possibly list everything that was so amazing about the trip and about Acadia National Park. We loved the breathtaking views from Cadillac Mountain, walking the perimeter of Jordan Pond after indulging in a lobster salad and popovers, hiking up Gorham Mountain, whale-watching and seeing Atlantic puffins. Being surrounded by God's creations every day was humbling and invigorating. We cannot say enough about Bar Harbor's friendly townspeople, or its wonderful art galleries, ice cream shops and restaurants. Of course, the people in the rooms of AA were most welcoming and helpful. It's a great destination for a sober getaway. We are currently planning our next trip because today we have a choice!

Diane S. and Carolyn H.
Warren, New Jersey

A drunk was driving through town with a carload of penguins. A policeman stopped the car. "You can't drive around like that. You better take those penguins to the zoo." The drunk promised he would, so the policeman let him go.

The next day the cop saw the same drunk driving around with the same load of penguins. This time they were all wearing sunglasses. The policeman pulled him over and said, "I thought you were going to take those penguins to the zoo."

"I did," said the drunk. "They had so much fun at the zoo that today I'm taking them to the beach."

December 1988

Fellowship on Ice
June 2016

As is often the case when it comes to AA lore, the origin of the The Coffee Cup hockey tournament has been the subject of a great deal of debate. There is no agreement on exactly who initiated the tournament or on what date the first game was played. There is some agreement, however, that the tournament started in the mid- to late-70s.

The general framework of The Coffee Cup history holds that a few AA guys from Sault Ste. Marie began playing hockey as a means of fellowship. At around the same time, a few AAs from Sudbury (one of them Bobby M.) gathered enough sober men to play hockey without beer in the dressing rooms. Word soon spread. The two factions were growing in numbers and in a typical display of alcoholic pride, the Sudbury squad challenged the "Soo" squad to a contest.

There were no formalities involved in those first games and it is uncertain whether the early teams consisted only of AA members. Family members and close friends of AA members may have played, and as the competition intensified over the years, it seems likely that "ringers" were imported. The games were serious and not without a few drops of blood spilled.

By the third or fourth year, North Bay AA put a team on the ice. By that time, the games had grown to a small tournament and The Coffee Cup was born. Soon after, Ottawa AA produced a team and each year a different city hosted the tournament. Over the years, teams formed and disbanded, but the core teams stayed together and are very much active today.

In 1989, a group of Hamilton AA men who played "shinny" together every Saturday night for years heard about the tournament. They joined in but were asked to leave the tournament after a bench-clearing brawl took place. But by Easter weekend of 1991 a new Hamilton team, put together by Marty C. and Ken D., traveled to Sault Ste. Marie to compete again, this time against the core teams as well as teams from Sudbury, Smith Falls, London, Timmins and Cornwall. Over the years, Hamilton's team has grown to more than 60 players of all ages, and several Hamilton women have joined the team.

The tournament that grew out of fellowship based on AA principles has lasted for 25 years and has kept growing all along. Each year, about 15 teams compete. Hamilton now has two teams. Ottawa has three teams, including players Marc J., Stevie and Frank. Sudbury has two teams, The Originals and the Nice Dogs, which is captained by Mario. The Smith Falls team includes 70-year-old Billy O., who can still be seen throwing elbows. Windsor and its captain Linc are mainstays. Toronto sends one or two very competitive teams, managed by Kelly K. The Brockville Bandits include

Lee E., Quinte and Dennis A., himself a transplanted Hamiltonian. There are teams from Kingston and Parry Sound. And one of our most significant teams is the Sobah Sistas, a group of women from all over the province who demonstrate a great love for the game and a "Why we are here" attitude like no other in the tournament.

A number of years ago, Hamilton played a team called Manotick in the finals of the Smith Falls tournament in an intense and penalty-filled game. Emotions ran high and the behavior on the ice began to look like anything but a spiritual endeavor. The goaltender for the Hamilton team waved the referees down and called the teams together in the middle of the game. It seemed like an unusual event in the heat of a championship game. The players looked around, puzzled, as did the referees, as the Hamilton players formed a circle at center ice inviting the Manotick players to join.

As the clock ran, the 30 players, joined by the non-AA referees, said the Serenity Prayer together. That created a tradition. Now, every game in the tournament includes a "Serenity Circle." When photos are taken of the game, there are more pictures of this circle than goals, saves, dekes and scraps combined.

The tournament is competitive. Without fail however, at the Saturday night banquet that comes at the end of the tournament, the power of AA fellowship that holds us all together is wonderfully apparent.

Friendships have been forged. We have watched families grow. We have suffered tragic loss together. When that subtle foe alcohol comes to claim one of our own, we band together as a team. We have watched men and women be attracted to the program of AA through the power of fellowship. We honor the Traditions and safeguard AA principles as we are constantly reminded that we have been spared. We are alive and participating, sober, in an amazing event and playing a game we love.

Marty C.
Hamilton, Ontario

The Best of Times

July 2007
From: Dear Grapevine

A s I approached my 30th anniversary, I reflected on what it was like, what happened, and what I am like now.

In 1990, I was living in San Diego. One weekend, nine AA friends and I went camping in the desert. We reserved a group camp-site at a state park and planned a campfire AA meeting after dinner. We also made great preparations to put on a "fashion review" after the meeting. Each person was to dress up as "what we were like."

What a spectacle! One guy had on a blue boa, another person wore pajamas, I wore one of my mother's hats, and so on. No one remembered to take a copy of the AA Preamble, so we all recited it in unison. Ten gay men in festive costumes chanted, "Alcoholics Anonymous is a Fellowship of men and women…" By the time we finished, a Marine and his wife walked up to our campsite. We thought we were going to be arrested, but he asked, "Is this an AA meeting?" (Have you ever seen a boa wilt?) We said, "Yes." The couple asked, "May we join you?" We said, "Of course."

I look back on difficult times in sobriety and I can say nothing bad ever happened to me—I was sober. Things do happen, and life takes its course. I am able to get through the tough times and I can look forward to the best of times because of AA.

Doug H.
Charlotte, North Carolina

Cruising Through the Jitters
August 2015

When I was eight years sober, one of my daughters was planning a big formal wedding, which would require my husband and me to accompany my mother-in-law to the east coast following the ceremony. The idea of both attending the wedding and traveling with my mother-in-law were daunting propositions at that point in my sobriety, so I discussed it with my sponsor, Helen. She said, "I know it's going to be difficult for you, Carolyn, but why not plan something nice for yourself afterward? My husband and I have enjoyed cruising at sea in our recovery. There are nice cruises originating on the east coast. Why not give it a try?"

I'm not sure which event was more anxiety-producing—the wedding or the idea of a cruise, but when I shared my sponsor's suggestion with my husband, he went right to work looking for cruises. In no time at all, he found a one-week cruise from New York to Montreal that was compatible with our wedding schedule. So with a mixture of excitement and dread, we booked it. As my sponsor had guessed, our time and attention were redirected toward planning, shopping and packing for our first cruise. The wedding became much less our concern.

I had always associated the idea of a cruise with a glamorous party scene including a lot of drinking, and it was hard to imagine myself in that setting without a drink in my hand. Helen said, "That's OK. Just make sure it's sparkling water."

We embarked at sunset and set sail down the Hudson River with a vivid sky reflected in the glass of the New York City skyline—a breathtaking beginning. I was filled with wonder and gratitude. I felt comfortable with my delicious sparkling water at the sail-away.

The next day at sea, I was surprised to discover that "Friends of Bill W." were meeting that afternoon in one of the many lounges. To my amazement, there were 11 recovering alcoholics present, many with far more time in recovery than I. We had a meeting and all exchanged cabin numbers at the end. It was extremely reassuring to see one another around the ship and on our tours. We all had the feeling that we had somehow "beaten the odds" for that day. We all made new friendships during the cruise, many of which have been long-lasting. Most importantly, all 11 of us stayed sober on that ship!

Carolyn S.
Gardnerville, Nevada

A group of us AA members gathered in a small conference room on the first day of an Alaskan cruise for a "Friends of Bill W." meeting. A gentleman stood outside the door, keeping his eye on us. Those inside had exchanged first names and had shaken hands—a sure sign we knew why we were there. When we asked the gentleman at the door if he would like to join us, he looked at us rather suspiciously and said, "I don't know. My name is Bill Wilson, and I would like to know who my friends are."

February 2005
Conrad B.

One S'more at a Time
August 2017

Kathleen and I waited in the parking lot. We said nervous greetings to people we had never met. Then we dropped our kayaks in the Saco River, in Brownfield, by the bridge. We anticipated an adventure. We were just not sure what that adventure would entail.

All of us on the trip that day had one thing in common—sobriety. Whoever said you can't have fun sober was wrong. We loved all of it, the paddling along the river, the community around the campfire and the conversation with Ron, a real Appalachian Trail through-hiker. These were just some of the things we enjoyed on the trip.

We were paddling with the flow of the river's current so there was not much struggle. We just floated downstream. Some people had canoes and offered to carry any supplies that would not fit into our smaller kayaks. I put my sunglasses on and pulled my sweatshirt off over my head. The initial social awkwardness turned into chatter as people started asking each other questions such as, "Where are you from?" and "Did you come on the trip last year?"

An iced tea sat in my cup holder where previously a beer would have sat. The banks of the river were mostly lined with coniferous trees. These strong, tall trees lined the uninhabited shore like a fence corralling us in.

I felt a sense of camaraderie among us 16 men and women on the river. We had all, at times in our lives, been on the same sinking ship. But we all had survived our life-threatening ordeal. Now we were floating down the river chatting, sharing snacks and laughing.

Two guys played guitar on their boat, the music echoing against a granite cliff downriver. After about four hours, we came up on a sandy beach and were waved in by fellow comrades. I climbed up the embankment to a grassy meadow where some from of our clan were spreading out tent tarps.

A huge maple tree stood with its canopy of branches and leaves hanging high in the sky over a circle of rocks that served as our community fire site. There were nine or so tents set up now. But no one made their own campfire. Instead, everyone congregated around a community fire pit. We all talked, cooked and sang. One girl even popped popcorn over the fire.

It was Saturday night. We had an AA meeting with the topic being gratitude. The amount of sober time people had ranged from a few weeks to a few decades, but no one was better than anyone else. All were allowed to speak, without judgment. All received equal respect.

On Sunday morning, a drizzle was making everything wet. But the smell of coffee brewing and blueberry pancakes and bacon sizzling got me out of the tent quickly.

Ron and I began chatting over his coffee percolator. He told me he had hiked the full Appalachian Trail from Springer Mountain, Georgia, all the way to Mount Katahdin, Maine, in five and a half months. Curious and intrigued, I began inquiring about his adventure. I listened intently as he spoke of fording rivers, enduring inclement weather, meeting hikers and townspeople.

He lit up talking about what he called "trail magic" happening, when he was the most desperate. Being a through-hiker on the Appalachian Trail has been a longtime dream of mine. Now that I am sober, that dream is a real possibility. We had so much fun kayaking sober on the river, interacting with others around the campfire and hearing about adventures hiking the Appalachian Trail.

When I saw the Hiram Bridge, I realized our "Serenity on the Saco" trip was coming to an end. As I pulled my kayak up onto the sandy shore, I felt sadness, knowing these strangers who I had so quickly become friends with would soon be departing.

I'm so glad I took plenty of photographs on the trip. I always find comfort in my photography because when faces and memories begin to fade, I have pictures to refresh my experiences.

Yesterday, the flyer came out for this summer's "Serenity on the Saco." There is no fee; all you need is willingness. Encouraging other newly sober people to come is my goal, so they will know we recovering alcoholics are not a glum lot.

Ellen D.
Auburn, Maine

Let's Do This
November 2016

I recently went on my first sober vacation. I traveled with seven other women from my home group to Turks and Caicos for a week. It was a beautiful place, so peaceful and serene; the water really was the color of turquoise. We laughed and cried together. There were many very special moments. We went to many AA meetings and heard stories of hope and recovery and the power of the program. We even had meetings at night on the beach, under the stars.

One of the things I wanted to do on this trip was to go horseback riding on the beach. My friend Christine and I signed up as soon as we got there. I had never been on a horse in my life. Horses are such beautiful animals and I had always been fascinated by them.

So off we went to the horse farm. We filled out all the paperwork. I stressed to the instructors that I was a beginner. I was feeling a little nervous. My old anxiety was creeping in. I have struggled with anxiety my entire life. It was especially crippling my first year of sobriety. I prayed about it a lot, asking my Higher Power for help. And to my amazement, it worked.

When the time came, the instructor helped me onto my horse. There it was again—the anxiety and fear. I began to cry. I told my instructor I wanted to get off. He assured me it would be OK. My friend Christine turned and looked at me; she saw my fear. She spoke very softly. "Lorraine," she said, "let it go." Over and over, she said this to me. I asked for help. I asked my Higher Power to remove my fear. It was a dream of mine to go horseback riding. I kept praying. And then it was gone; my fear was gone. My tears were gone. I said, "OK, I'm ready. Let's do this."

I had the most amazing and spiritual experience. My horse was a very gentle soul. We went down some trails. And then at the bottom of the trail, I saw the sand and the ocean before us. I rode my horse into the ocean. She loved it and so did I.

I will never forget this experience. Through the Fellowship of AA and my Higher Power I had a beautiful sober vacation.

The first thing I did when I got home was to sign up for horseback riding lessons. It is truly amazing the life that has been given to me— as long as I trust in my Higher Power.

Lorraine M.
Clinton, Connecticut

Fireflies, Ghost Stories and Campfire Coffee
April 2021

Our cars pulled up to Trout Pond and we hiked back along the lake to the campsite. We pitched our tents around the campfire site like alcoholics circling up for an AA meeting. The moon, stars and fireflies reflected on the water as we held hands and said the Serenity Prayer hand in hand. Newly blossoming sober trans femmes began to take turns tending the fire.

Later, we invoked and celebrated the presence of each of our Higher Powers huddled around a common fire where we sang songs and told ghost stories. We got to witness the wide eyes of a newcomer grateful not to be drinking as he curled up next to the dry firewood near one of the biggest of the tents.

We also got to see an alcoholic being introduced to AA literature at our morning meeting as they chose "A Vision For You" to be read over our campfire coffee. There was exuberance in the air as the gay crowd one by one identified as transgender drunks sitting around enjoying each other's fellowship at our yearly camping adventure. We used inclusive language to make way for and support our fellow alcoholics in need of an AA meeting that is safe.

Then later we celebrated sober birthdays as we helped a new swimmer across the lake to the sunny side to rest in the sunshine of the spirit. We held a meditation meeting while half-dipped in the lake on the sun-speckled rocks.

On our final day, birds, deer, snakes, butterflies, frogs, fishes and even fairies showed up in our gratitude circles as we prepared to do service and break camp, leaving the pond site better than we found it. We even had an AA meeting at a diner on our way back to Brooklyn.

I'm so grateful our trans AA fellowship called me into a new life of love and service. Here's to our Trout Pond adventure. Until next year.

Lucky M.
Brooklyn, New York

A drinker finds his cohort at the bar, staring down into his glass of beer, gaze fixed in astonished horror. "What are you doing," asks the first, "drowning your sorrows?"

"Trying to," admits the glum one, "but the damn things can swim!"

October 1990
Bill C., Downey, California

In Good Company
June 2016

t was Memorial Day weekend 1991. I was 38 years old at the time, two years sober, and quite happy about it all. The initial fog had started to lift, and it seemed like God had given me the world wrapped in a red bow and said, "Go. Enjoy. Just don't drink."

One thing I had always wanted to do was whitewater rafting, even though I knew not one thing about it. But that's what a phone is for, right? I picked out a rafting place at random from the phone book and called for information. It sounded easy enough. I would dress comfortably, show up at the river and be put in a group of other rafters.

But I ran into a problem. Despite my "carpe diem" sweatshirt and easy smile, I could not find one solitary soul, in the program or out of it, to go with me on my Memorial Day rafting adventure. So the trip would be my first adventure alone and sober. I was scared. But sobriety is all about new experiences, isn't it? So I decided to go anyway, with only my Higher Power to accompany me.

In my short time in AA, I had been given many examples of how a Higher Power worked in my life. And I listened when people in the program said, "Nothing, absolutely nothing, in God's world happens by mistake."

So with joy in my heart, gas in my car and an empty passenger seat at my side, I set off for Ohiopyle, a trip of about two hours, to do what I had dreamed of doing for 20 years. I turned to the empty seat and said, "This is great." The seat said nothing.

Showing up at Ohiopyle, I pulled into the large unpaved parking lot surrounded on all sides by various kiosk-type huts selling rafting trips. While looking for a spot to park, I noticed several cars with bumper stickers that said, "Higher Powered," "One Day At A Time" and "Friend Of Bill." What were the chances?

So I set out to find the hut with the most alcoholic-looking people I could find. At that point in my recovery I figured I could probably tell by looking. I settled on a hut and was assigned to a rafting group. Were any of these the AA bumper sticker people?

Our guide from the hut outfitted us with helmets and lifejackets and gave us our six-person raft. We were assigned seats on the raft, with me sitting in the front-right spot. Instructions were given, rafting skills explained, and once we were in our raft and practicing in the river, lots of inadvertent paddling in circles and raucous laughter followed. Imagine that, I thought. I can actually have fun with "earth people" too. Since most of my time until that point in recovery had been spent with people from the program, this was a new experience in more ways than one.

Off we went to begin our trek down the river. The first set of rapids approached. When we got to it, one person fell out of the raft. It was not me. We regrouped. The second set of rapids approached, and one person dropped their oar in the water. It was not me. Again, we regrouped. The third set of rapids approached, and we got stuck on the rock. And, yes, it was me who got stuck. But we regrouped.

By the time we approached the fourth set of rapids, we were laughing together like the seasoned rafting veterans we felt ourselves to be. I had long since given up my efforts to figure out who among our rafting crew, if any, was a drunk like me—although my money would have been on Mr. Back Left.

The fourth set of rapids was challenging. It had lots of obstacles, lots of whitewater and lots of big rocks. But none of us fell out. No one lost an oar. We steered clear through. But we went over backwards. Laughing. And Miss Middle Left said, "Well, you know what they say, 'It's progress, not perfection.'"

Time stopped. Could it be? Was she the drunk I had been seeking? And if so, how would I go about letting her know I was one too? I couldn't just ask, "Are you a drunk like me?" What if she wasn't? And then there was the anonymity thing. I thought about dropping a hint, like saying, "One paddle at a time." Better to just be silent and wait till lunch, I decided, at which point I cornered Miss Middle Left where I could not be overheard.

"Hey, I liked what you said back there, that 'progress, not perfection' thing." I said. "Where did you ever get that from?" I thought I was being pretty smooth. "Well," she answered, "I just heard it around." Wow, I thought, earth people used terms like that too. But then, after a short pause, she added, "... around the rooms."

I was stunned and started excitedly talking. "Oh my gosh," I said, "I'm also in the program and I saw all those bumper stickers in the parking lot. I thought there might be a drunk out here somewhere. But I never would have guessed that you..." Babbling at its finest. She stopped me and said, "Yes, I am in the program. As a matter of fact, everyone in our raft is in the program. Except for that newlywed couple over there, all 60 of us in this group are in the program."

My mouth fell open and she excitedly walked back toward the group yelling, "Hey everyone! Holly here is a friend of Bill's too!" And in true AA fashion, I was welcomed with open arms into the group of drunks who had traveled up that day from Maryland. I spent the rest of the trip with my new friends, laughing and paddling and enjoying the special fellowship that is found in AA. At the end of the trip down the river they invited me back to their campsite, where we shared a wonderful dinner outdoors and an AA meeting around the campfire.

Just like they say in the Big Book, I was right where I needed to be. What were the chances of me going on a rafting trip by myself and ending up on that day, at that particular time, at that kiosk, so that I got to raft with that group?

There was no doubt in my mind that day that my Higher Power was looking after me. It was almost as if there was writing in the sky, saying something like, "Don't worry Holly, I've got it under control."

Holly H.
Altoona, Pennsylvania

A newcomer was showing a friend his garden, the first he had ever planted. The friend noticed several small green clusters at one end of the plot and asked curiously what they were.

"Radishes," said the newcomer.

"How interesting," commented his friend. "Most gardeners plant them in rows."

"They do?" puzzled the newcomer. "That seems strange. They always come in bunches at the store."

August 1987

Grabbing the Gold
April 2021

Sobriety has been good to me. I now live a life I only dreamed of and often fantasized about from a barstool. One example of my good fortune is spending days floating in the middle of Puget Sound, crabbing from my boat.

I have crabbed on a regular basis since I was 15. And I always dreamed of the day when I could be in the middle of the Sound, spending all day letting the sun warm my skin, waiting for the Dungeness gold that would surely be in the pots as I pulled them at the end of the day.

That day never arrived when I was drinking. One chaotic situation after another seemed to be the routine, and the years just passed by. Occasionally, I'd throw a ring pot off the end of a pier and tell the other people on the pier how someday I would be "out there" with the big boys grabbing the gold. As you might imagine, I would tell these tales between swigs of brown-bagged beer and a puff of this or that. The last three years of my drinking I did no crabbing at all. Trying to stay out of jail and keeping a job occupied all my time.

I finally did get sober and I have stayed sober, thanks to God and AA and the people in it. As the sober days turned into weeks, the weeks turned into months and the months into years, I was once again throwing a ring pot off the end of a pier and thinking of being "out there." Could the program that saved my life and repatriated me back into society make my dream come true? I had seven years of sobriety and I thought to myself, Let's see what God has in store for you.

It was the beginning of another year and tax returns would be coming soon. I had always put any return I received back into my house as a principal payment against the mortgage, but this year I decided to do something different. If it was to be, I would take my $3500 tax refund and try to buy a boat. It took two months, but the happy day did arrive, and I became the proud owner of a 17-foot-long V boat with a 140-horsepower motor. Good enough to be "out there" on a calm day. I could also use it for fishing lakes and tubing.

Since that day in March of 2011, I've had so many wonderful days on the water. My son was 14 then and he has many lifetime memories of tubing with his friends, catching salmon in Humpy Hollow off the coast of Mukilteo and catching crab like they were going out of style.

There was no way I was going to keep this wonderful gift to myself. I often invited people from my AA meetings to come out with me for a day on the water. Some were not interested but many were, and I was able to share the experience with them.

"You have to pull your own pots if you want to take some home," I'd say in a boat-captain voice, adding, "Faith without works is dead." We'd all laugh and somehow we all knew that the greatest days of our existence were right then, with the sun warming our skin and stunning views all around and so many stories of experience, strength and hope to share. The crab feasts later in the evening only added to the experience. Crab, potatoes, corn on the cob, bibs and mallets for everyone! The stories would continue into the night and usually we wound up in a meeting to tell fish tales to all the other members.

I've heard a few Fifth Steps "out there" as well, and have in return become closer to people than I ever thought possible. Today it feels good to do good. The more this way of life gives me, the more I try to share it and give it away to others. It's only because of AA and the Fellowship that these wonderful experiences on the water were able to happen for me at all.

I recently gave my boat to a lifelong friend I've known since I was 15. He and his family are sober now and I want them to be able to experience all the things my family has gotten to experience.

I have to pass on the message of AA to the still-suffering alcoholic. I believe that I can pass along the gifts that I've been given to all those trying to live a better life too. Besides, most of my AA brothers, including my sponsor, have motorcycles and take frequent trips and rides together now. So since I've passed along my boat, I guess a motorcycle might be next on my list!

Curt W.
Lake Stevens, Washington

CHAPTER FIVE

Going Places

Planes, trains, ships and laptops—traveling the globe
without a drink

From New York to Paris, the Alps to Kilimanjaro and Virginia to the Australian outback, alcoholics who formerly "dug a groove" in their sofas, as Tom C. memorably puts it in his story "Gettin' Busy," hit the road for the sheer pleasure of expanding their horizons sober.

For AAs hungering for a meeting, there's nothing like the sheer pleasure of discovering one in an unexpected place. In "Surprise Picnic in the Wilderness," Renee J. and her husband find themselves in Kentucky while taking a road trip across the country. It's her ninth sober anniversary—and no meetings in sight. But to their surprise, an AA sign in a remote spot leads them to a sober picnic where members welcome them with open arms. "The memories we have from that day will always be with us," Renee writes. "The people we met will never be forgotten, nor will the huge welcome we received."

"In sobriety," writes Nicola M. in her story "No Grappa For You," "one of my healthiest cravings is for travel and adventure." Booking a two-week hiking and cycling trip in Slovenia was indeed adventurous. Nicola fends off Germans proffering blueberry brandy and an insistent waiter who wants to put a dollop of grappa in her mint tea—until she finally tells him she is sober. ("No grappa for you!" he exclaims.) The highlight of the trip is the meeting in Ljubljana where people speak only Slovene, but Nicola knew she was in the right place. She got to act out her share with "a version of AA charades." "I patted my heart," she writes, "and let them know that what I needed most was for my heart to connect with their hearts."

Virtual traveling also brings joys and surprises as expressed in the article "My Friends in the Outback." During the 2020 pandemic, writer Terrie S. joins meetings on virtual platforms from her home in Virginia and discovers—as have so many AAs—the pleasures of exploring AA in other countries right from her home. She finds a wonderful women's meeting in Alice Springs, Australia. After making friends there, she attends the virtual 55th Australian National Convention in Toowoomba, Queensland. Half-measures avail Terrie nothing: "I went so far as to move into the guest room of our apartment. I slept during the day and went to meetings during the early mornings. I even walked my dogs on Australian time!"

As the stories in this chapter show, sober alcoholics, traveling the world virtually or otherwise, can find AA almost anywhere they go and join in on the fun, companionship and fellowship—all reminders that "we aren't a glum lot."

Far from it.

Sober in Paris
September 1979

I t was my first trip alone, after five years in AA, and I was going to Paris. I had visited Paris in my drinking days, and drunken memories remained with me. I had been known as *le buveur* (the drinker). In my five years in AA, I had been transformed from a drunken, nearly penniless, irresponsible hack artist into a competent illustrator painter. This trip, sober, I was to sketch and paint the beauty of Paris.

I arrived in Paris exhausted from the all-night trip, and the next day checked my address book for the English-speaking AA meeting. It read: "Quai d'Orsay, Eglise Américaine, open meeting, 5:00 PM." Impulsively (impulsiveness is one of my character defects), I crossed over to the Left Bank. I found the street, but no church. I asked a gendarme for directions in my broken French, and I was pointed in the direction of Pont d'Allessandre. A half hour later, I limped into the AA meeting.

It was as if I discovered an oasis in the Sahara Desert. When I told those AAs I had just blown in from New York, I was warmly welcomed. Chairing the meeting was an expatriate painter from the States, who has lived in Paris for nearly 30 years. And to my surprise, a New York AA friend, Sandy, was sitting at the table. After the meeting, he asked me if I was going for coffee. Of course, there's no better way to get to know people than at an AA coffee klatch. Around the table in the cafe were my friend Sandy, a Scottishwoman, an American, two Englishmen, and a Frenchwoman—quite a United Nations of AA!

From then on my trip was smooth sailing. I now had sightseeing and dinner companions. Charlie, the American painter, invited some of us to his studio for coffee, and told me to call if I needed any help or information. The next day I spotted another AA friend from New

York on the street. He wanted to know where the AA meeting was, and I was able to help him. It's a small world if you're in AA.

One night I returned to my hotel room late after our evening AA coffee klatch, and checked the money I had left in my traveling case. I found I had been robbed, and the thief had taken everything except two American pennies. Even an active alcoholic couldn't have gotten drunk on that! I was in a foreign country with only two pennies to my name. Although I was upset, I didn't panic. I thought over my options, said a prayer to my Higher Power and went to sleep.

The next morning I reported the theft to the concierge, and to my surprise, he lent me 500 francs. Next I called Charlie, who reminded me that my bank has a branch in Paris and told me how to get there. I took my problem to the bank, and within three days my money arrived from New York. So the only hitch in my vacation was taken care of very easily, with help from my friends.

My trip was filled with wonderful dinners at the French restaurants, a meeting at the studio of another American painter who is in the program, the ballet, concerts, painting in the Bois de Boulogne—all with my AA friends. I came home with 50 sketches and five paintings, saw and did twice as much in Paris, sober, in two weeks as I did in a month when I was drinking—enjoyed it, too! So if you go to Paris, don't miss the AA meeting at the Eglise Américaine. It's one of the unsung pleasures of Paris.

P. K.
New York, New York

Look Out for Two Old Ladies
May 2013

My favorite friend and I met way back on a bright fall day in the mid-70s. We were fresh teenagers wearing peasant outfits while working at the local steakhouse. I don't know who thought of the idea first, but we found that work was extremely fun with tumblers full of rum and coke hidden in our hostess stand. We bonded over those and many, many other alcoholic moments. It was fun—and disastrous.

Over the years, my friend Christine and I appeared to live parallel self-destructive lives. We moved to Arizona and both found dead-end relationships. I eventually came back to my hometown in 1985. I had heard of AA through my mother's attempt to get sober. I thought if she could do it, then maybe I could too.

At 27 years old, I found myself living at home. I was so delusional I thought I had to hide my liquor from family members, but nobody ever even seemed interested in finding it, let alone taking it away from me. After I got sober I came to find out many alcoholics hide their liquor—even when there is no one around to find or touch it. It took many attempts, a lot of one-on-one sessions with a sober therapist, and getting down on my knees a few times, before sobriety finally saved me in October 1985.

A few years later, my best friend also eventually returned to our hometown with her baby daughter. We ran into each other after losing contact for those few years. I was able to tell her of my sobriety. She congratulated me and gave me a big hug. Shortly thereafter I got a call from her. She was interested in checking out AA. It stuck for her right away, and she found her sobriety in February of 1988. Since that time we have both enjoyed continuous sobriety.

The best part of having my best friend sober with me is that we both love to travel, laugh, shop and get pampered—things better off done with a great friend, instead of a husband who doesn't quite understand the finer feelings of enjoying a great cup of coffee while soaking your feet in a pedicure tub and yakking away with your buddy.

Through following directions from our sponsors and other strong women in the program, Christine was able to raise a wonderful daughter. Rachel grew up in AA meetings; first in a carrier, then a stroller and finally with crayons and coloring books in tow. My support system saw me through an associate's degree, a bachelor of arts and finally a master's degree. Through diligence and love, both of us have sober lives filled with many of the Promises. It has afforded us jobs we like and the ability to travel. We don't go on luxury cruises or five-star tours, but we do find inexpensive ways to have fun. She lives on the West Coast and I live on the East Coast. About once or twice a year we plan an excursion to a different city for shopping, walking and touring. We've met in Portland for great food, Santa Fe for beautiful weather, Tucson and Sedona for sunshine and shopping, Chicago for stunning architecture and Las Vegas for a show of her favorite comedian. Anytime you travel with Christine she'll pull out her comedy CDs and get the laughter started quickly.

I'm a hiker, skier, dog-and-cat kind of person; Christine is more of the art-festivals-in-the-city type of woman. But she is definitely more adventurous than I am. She'll find coupons for a luxury stay in Thailand and go off on an adventure of her own. A few years ago she finally convinced me that getting a passport wasn't a challenging ordeal. She told me fear was only "false evidence appearing real" and that I should go for it. I did. Little did I know I would soon find myself eating bologna sandwiches at 3 A.M. (San Francisco time), as we flew to Sydney, Australia. If you want to have a great time in sobriety, find a kangaroo to feed! It's fantastic. Try to get your best friend to stand next to a huge peacock and take her picture. Or even better, if you find yourself in Arizona, try to get her to go stand by a wild brahma bull. Tell her it will make a great holiday photo.

Christine and I have known each other for 35 years; combined we have over 50 years of sobriety. Things that appear to keep us young are cheap trips, thrift shops, much laughter and a thorough enjoyment and appreciation for our sobriety. We both still go to meetings, have sponsors and work strong programs. We both also have very busy careers and lives with our families.

It's one of the most calming and enjoyable parts of my life to know I have someone to call who always has my back and who can always make me laugh. Find a friend, enjoy sobriety and find a museum, walking path or a park bench. Enjoy a great cup of coffee, some one-to-one fellowship and wonderful laughter. And if you find yourself in Belize this holiday season, look out for two old ladies—one will be trying to convince the other that baboons and howler monkeys at the sanctuary will make a great picture—if she would just move in a little closer!

Helen H.
Pittsburgh, Pennsylvania

I surprised my wife of 39 years with a trip to Venice. One night at a posh restaurant she ordered a glass of very fine wine. Sipping, she remarked on how wonderful it was. My alcoholic hand reached over to taste. I caught myself and thought, Man, do I need a meeting!

On returning to the hotel, I asked the concierge if he could do something important for me. I asked him to find me an AA meeting. I explained, "You know, a meeting of Alcoholics Anonymous."

He looked at me pityingly, and said gently and slowly, "Signor, this is Italy; you can drink anywhere."

May 2006
Evan Q., Laredo, Texas

No Grappa For You!
May 2011

I n sobriety, one of my healthiest cravings is for travel and adventure. Recently, I booked a two-week hiking and cycling trip to Slovenia. When I checked the AA website for Slovenia, I discovered it to be entirely in Slovene, using the Cyrillic alphabet. So I emailed the AA international office and received a response from Trevor in Italy. He told me there was no definite info for meetings, but he did have an address for a possible meeting and two phone numbers.

I set off with my smartphone loaded up with the audio version of the Big Book, some speaker CDs, a few Grapevines and a lot of prayer.

The Julian Alps border Slovenia and Northern Italy. The country is devoid of pollution and the hiking was incredible. I sent my sponsor a photo of a mountain we climbed and she sent a message back asking, "Did you touch the hand of God?" Some of the hiking was so extreme, that I not only touched the hand of God, I reached out and grabbed it, praying out loud as I heaved myself over a vertical cliff face and rolled onto a tiny grass plateau at the peak. On top of this particular mountain, there were three Germans who greeted me with applause and offered to share their flask of brandy. Another day, at a mountain hut beside an Alpine lake, we were offered a tray of homemade blueberry brandy shots. One morning, I had a bit of a tummy ache and the hotel made me fresh mint tea as a soothing agent. The waiter sidled up to me conspiratorially and said, "What really works is grappa. Let me get you some grappa. Really, grappa is what you need."

I smiled and politely declined all these various offers everywhere I went, but this waiter was insistent. Finally, I looked at him and said, "I have not had a drink for 14 years, 11 months and five days, today."

It seems that there is a universal understanding that if someone is counting days from alcohol, there must be a good reason. The waiter stood up straight and loudly proclaimed, "No grappa for you!"

My smartphone tracked my progress via text messages: "Welcome to Italy," "Welcome to Austria," and "Welcome to Croatia." Cycling through the river valley on the Croatian border was breathtaking. The water was so clear, mirror images of the landscapes reflected the whole way. As Slovenian maps bear little relation to Slovenian roads, there were some testing times when some of the cyclists felt the need to double-guess the kindness of strangers and the directions we were given. My solution was to keep my mouth shut and volunteer to go scout the alternate route in question. So I'd cycle off and explore, come back and report a dead end so we could all continue as directed.

I was reading my Grapevines and emailing my AA buddies, but after 13 days, I was really missing my meetings. I prayed for comfort and God gifted me with the opposite of drunk dreams. I started dreaming that I was in AA meetings. On the last cycling day, I woke up with a clear recollection of having been in marathon meetings all night long. I had one day back in Ljubljana before we flew out, so I called the two numbers Trevor had given me. Neither were in use. The meeting times he had given me were for Tuesdays and Thursdays. This was a Wednesday, so I asked the hotel if I could use their computer, and discovered one English–speaking meeting listed on the U.S. Embassy website for a Wednesday night. I studied some online maps, but the click boxes were also in Slovene. Somehow, I managed to find a map showing that the meeting address was only two kilometers from my hotel. I went down to the coffee bar and asked the guys if the map I had was accurate. They all spoke some English and drew an alternate walking route for me and I set off to see if the meeting existed.

Following the directions to number 14, the location listed was a huge apartment building. So where would the AA meeting be? I headed around back and looked for a basement, walked down some steps and straight into a locked doorway with AA and Al-Anon meeting schedules attached to the door. I took a photo of the schedule, returned to the coffee bar and showed the guys the picture, asking for clarification. "Sreda" was Wednesday. The meeting was scheduled for 7 P.M.

I cannot tell you how excited I was when I went back that night. I arrived early and the meeting room was open. It was a clubhouse with two meeting rooms, a kitchenette and a restroom. The Steps, Traditions and Serenity Prayer, all in Slovene, hung from the wall alongside pictures of Bill and Bob and a stack of anonymity cards on a small table. I felt like dancing. Four people arrived, none of whom spoke English. We established that I was an alcoholic and definitely in the right pace. I stayed and listened to an hour of Slovenian sharing. A newcomer sat with her arms crossed until she must have heard something that made it clear to her that she was in the wrong place and she stomped out. I made a prayer sign in her direction and we all nodded. They let me share in English and a bit of French and I played a version of AA charades by acting out my share. I mimed climbing mountains, being offered booze and politely declining. We all laughed and I patted my heart and let them know that what I needed most was for my heart to connect to their hearts. One lady said haltingly, "I understand," and spoke to the other two in Slovene. They all patted their hearts. We closed the meeting with the Serenity Prayer, once in Slovenian, then again in English, and we all hugged.

The language of the heart transcends all other languages. The tourist board of Slovenia makes T shirts, hats and mugs with the appropriate slogan, "I feel Slovenia."

Thanks to AA and a God of my understanding, I truly felt your love, Slovenia, and I am so grateful.

Nicola M.
Laguna Niguel, California

Surprise Picnic in the Wilderness
May 2011
Online Exclusive

In 2009, my husband and I were traveling on a well-deserved vacation from our home in the Colorado Rocky Mountains back East to see his family. We had just spent a week with them and had a wonderful time. We found ourselves in Nashville, Tennessee and decided to get to a meeting to celebrate my nine-year anniversary in the AA program. We looked up available meetings online as we now do regularly on vacations, and found very few actually posted online in the Nashville area. We did find one that we could make it to, and we set off to find our meeting.

When we arrived in the general area, some type of festival was going on and streets were blocked off in every direction. We decided to just park on the outskirts and walk to the meeting. As we drove around we started to notice the kind of neighborhood we were in... very rough and scary. If we went to the meeting it would mean walking back to our car in the dark around 9:30 P.M. We also had some of our belongings strapped to the roof of our car in a storage container and decided it would not be a good idea to leave our car or our things in this neighborhood. Every time we reconsidered just parking and going, a strong feeling inside of me would indicate that this was not a good idea. We reluctantly went back to our hotel room with no meeting.

The following day, which happened to be Labor Day, we set off for the Kentucky border. We had been attending AA meetings all along our journey, so we had quickly bounced back from not being able to attend the meeting the night before. As I was driving down the highway, my husband suddenly said, "Exit here so we can go see the lakes." I pulled off the highway and onto a two-lane road. We drove a few miles and realized that we had missed the turn we wanted to take to get to the lake. We decided to go down a little further and do a U-turn. As we approached our intersection to turn around, I just about drove off the road when I spotted an AA sign with an arrow pointing left! I asked my husband if that could possibly be "our AA." We decided to follow the signs to whatever was going on to find out. We saw a parking area with a little pavilion right next to the lake and pulled in. There we spotted people setting up for some kind of picnic. Without even really making a conscious decision, we quickly parked and got out of our car. We walked toward the pavilion and were immediately greeted with "Hi!" And "Hello!"

I sat down next to a woman who first greeted us and within minutes found out that this was "our AA." We had stumbled on the Western Kentucky Intergroup Picnic and that we were welcome to stay. You would think we had won the lottery. We immediately started chatting with everyone there, doing introductions and just enjoying the company of the kind of people we feel comfortable with. We felt we had known these people all of our AA lives and were welcomed with open arms. We were not only invited to stay for the Intergroup meeting, but to stay for the picnic that followed and the speaker that afternoon. That meant we would be there for about six hours. We decided to go for it. What a great decision that was.

My husband shared our experience of our Nashville meeting attempt and that it was also my 9th AA birthday. The next thing I knew, people were coming up and congratulating me from all sides. I felt like a celebrity!

We stayed for the Intergroup meeting and were given business cards with the group's information so we could stay in touch. We were given a copy of their bylaws to take back to Colorado and share with our groups. One member even loaded us up with fresh canned preserves and hot peppers he had recently acquired and still had in his car.

Soon the picnic began and more people showed up. We had a wonderful meal and great conversation with everyone. We had a chance to talk with the speaker for the day who was the DCM for the area. She shared that she had just come home from a business trip the day before and was exhausted, but still drove the two hours to speak at our picnic. When it came time for her speech, the first thing she did was talk about a couple from Colorado who had shown up at the picnic and how much it meant to her. She said it reenergized her to know we were there when she was at a point of near exhaustion. I couldn't believe she was talking about us! Then she caught me by total surprise when she called me to the front to present my nine-year chip to me. I was floored! I can't really put into words the way I was feeling...almost like being in a dream.

We had found our AA meeting that we missed the night before. God had closed one door and opened a much bigger one the next day. It was a great reminder that things happen in his time, not mine. The memories we have from that day will always be with us. The people we met will never be forgotten, nor will the huge welcome we received.

A couple of days later we attended a 7:00 A.M. meeting in Kansas. We got the same kind of welcome there! We each received a "keep coming back" welcome chip and they wanted to give me another nine-year chip. We were invited to breakfast after the meeting and had a wonderful time.

We have tried vacations with no meetings and found it to be a huge mistake. We thought we were too busy to go to meetings...this was our time to relax and have fun. We ended up stressed out and at each other's throats in a very short period of time. Today our meetings are a part of our vacations—a big part! We attended meetings in several areas on our trip and the result was a sober and sane vacation together. We met all kinds of new friends along the way. This experience has inspired me to come home and start attending different meetings that may be a little further away but that will be a new experience for me. I am forever grateful that AA is in just about every corner of the world. We may have to drive a ways, but it's well worth the time.

Renee J.
Divide, Colorado

My Friends in the Outback
September 2021

My husband has 39 years of sobriety and I have 31. We had established our "nonnegotiable" Friday date nights about the same time I started attending virtual meetings in Alice Springs, Australia. Little did I know, when I first pushed the "join" button to the Alice Springs meetings, how my life would be forever changed and enriched by a group so far away.

My husband and I live in Alexandria, Virginia. During the pandemic, I had to learn new technology skills to attend online AA meetings. I had just barely learned how to text my grandchildren on my smartphone and now I had to learn how to log onto meetings on my computer pad.

Once I became comfortable with daily meetings, I began to explore AA meetings in different states and then, to my surprise, meetings in other countries! I was intrigued by a small women's meeting I found in Australia on Saturday mornings. Due to time zone differences, I had to log in on Friday nights to attend.

At first, my husband and I continued our date nights by starting out for the restaurant a little earlier. I would have my dessert wrapped and ready to go home for the meeting. Eventually, we decided that this meeting was more important than our date nights.

Once I clicked on the meeting link to Alice Springs, I noticed the Steps and Traditions were posted on the wall. The meeting was not in somebody's house, but in a conference room in a hospital. I started to relax when I heard the familiar words of the Preamble and "How It Works," even if some of the words were pronounced a little funny. I knew I was home.

Each week, the ladies of Alice Springs welcomed me, and slowly I assimilated to a different way of stating my sobriety date and a few slang words and phrases. I soon realized that the AA message is the same in Alice Springs as it is in Alexandria or, for that matter, Cleveland or San Francisco.

As we shared our common experiences in our struggles to stay sober, other ladies joined us and got caught up in our eagerness to help the newcomer get sober. I admit I was slightly jealous when the Aussies could share phone numbers and I couldn't. Long distance phone calls, especially overseas calls, would put a crimp in our budget.

That problem changed when I became friends with several of the ladies in the group on social media. I will never forget my first international phone call through my computer. I even switched over to "video chats."

At first I was apprehensive about what these chats would do to our monthly phone bill, but I soon realized that our phone and internet were two separate bills and now I am free to talk with anybody in another country without worrying about the cost. That rocketed me into another dimension alright. And getting acquainted with the gorgeous landscape of Australia and its animals through my new friends was frosting on the cupcake of fellowship.

But the most influential experience of my sobriety, besides doing my Fourth and Fifth Steps, was attending the virtual 55th Australian National Convention in Toowoomba, Queensland, that October. A buddy from Alice Springs and I wondered why we had to pay $100 for a virtual convention when there really shouldn't be any expense, and I must admit that I had very low expectations. Most of my experiences at conventions had involved meeting people in person and I didn't have any idea how I would meet anybody there virtually. Boy was I wrong!

I committed myself to getting all I could out of my $100 investment. I went so far as to move into the guest room of our apartment with the intention of living on Australian time during the conference. I slept during the day and went to meetings during the early mornings. I even walked my dogs on Australian time!

I was pleased to find that the conference was well-organized.

There were preconvention videos, as well as opportunities to set up a personal profile complete with video, biographical sketch and contact information. I did have a little trouble remembering the password "Toowoomba," as I kept changing the letters to Wootoomba. With a little practice, the spelling became second nature to me.

I was impressed with the convention from beginning to end. The organization and planning were phenomenal. Talks by Alateens, Al-Anons and AA members were inspiring. There was even a virtual play, a drama featuring the characters of Bill and Lois. We played a game called "Kahoot!" that tested knowledge of the Australian history of AA, and it kept my head spinning. I was so glad that I had the foresight to bring a notebook to take notes. I loved the virtual tour of Toowoomba. I felt like I was on a tour bus with all of my Aussies, driving on the wrong side of the road.

One of the best experiences was hearing a talk given by a Jesuit from New York named Father Bill. He told the tale of the early history of AA and the Oxford Group. He summarized the Twelve Steps and ended with the moving prayer that has had a deep impact on my spiritual life. Something changed inside of me as I heard the "Step Aside" prayer for the first time. Now I say it weekly with a prayer buddy.

When the conference souvenir book arrived in the mail, I was blown away by the history of how AA came to Australia. But I never got past a superficial thumbing of the book because of an insert that fell out of it. It was the recipe for Lamington cake, which I had heard so much about.

I immediately set out on a mission to assemble the ingredients and my husband and I made the cake. But there was one problem I didn't see beforehand: the metric system! Now I had to learn the temperature of the oven and how much butter to put in. Our cake didn't turn out like the one in the photo however, and if I ever get to Australia, that cake is one of the first things I will order.

It may seem hard to believe, but I now consider Alice Springs to be my new home group, even though it's on the other side of the world.

With the close-knit fellowship of such a small group, we have gotten to know each other on a very personal level.

I have even been able to provide service to the group as host and cohost. I practice the Seventh Tradition by contributing to the GSO in the name of the Darwin district, and we all carry the AA message to fellow alcoholics the world over.

Terrie S.
Alexandria, Virginia

Out on a road trip, an elderly alcoholic couple stops at a roadside bar for lunch. They have a few and get back on the road. After driving a while, the woman realizes she's left her glasses on the table. By then, they have to travel quite a distance before they can turn around. The man fusses and complains all the way back to the bar. He just won't let up one minute. Finally they arrive, and as the woman gets out of the car to retrieve her glasses, the old geezer yells, "While you're in there, you might as well get my hat!

January 2004
Richard M.

Gettin' Busy
January 2019

For a while there, I thought August 14, 2011 would go down as the worst day of my life.

The previous day, I launched my morning with a spiked coffee and then alternated the rest of the day between white wine and beer. I wasn't trying to get drunk. My goal was only to feed a steady, daylong buzz. Despite my goal, 15 hours later I got lost after stumbling out of a friend's house three blocks from my own doorstep.

I woke the next morning hungover and humiliated, but finally ready to acknowledge I'd lost the ability to control my drinking. I cringed at the thought of having to say aloud, "Hi, I'm Tom and I'm an alcoholic." But I knew it was time to openly admit I had a problem. That day in August would be the day I decided I'd had enough. I had hit my bottom.

Or so I thought. A worse day awaited me.

On day 7, my first sober Saturday, I woke up and realized glumly I had nothing to do and nothing to occupy my time. While never a barfly, I'd spent most of the past year moldering on the couch with a drink in my right hand and the remote control in my left. Drinking wasn't an option anymore, but I had nothing else to fill the long hours before me.

As I applied the shaving cream that awful morning, staring back at me in the mirror was an absolute bore. Worse even than being a drunk was having to admit alcohol had made me an empty shell of a human being.

Desperate for something to divert me from the liquor cabinet, I threw myself into cleaning the house. By late morning I had washed and folded four loads of laundry and had the place shining. My poor wife, trying to relax on her day off, was ready to pull her hair out. "Could you please sit still?" she asked, exasperated.

I admitted, pathetically, that I could not. Two choices lay before me: Find something to busy myself with or start drinking again. By the skin of my teeth, I stayed sober that day, but I knew things couldn't go on like this.

I reluctantly began attending AA meetings and racked my brain for hobbies that had once interested me. This was more difficult than you might expect. My alcoholic brain moved slowly then. Gradually however, I recalled that I once enjoyed cooking. There had always been music playing in my house and I used to like to read.

As I labored through those early days sober, I dusted off my cookbooks, dug out old records and hit the library. I was nothing more than a dry drunk but at least there were good smells and sounds coming from my kitchen. I could bury myself in a novel rather than a bottle. Over time, I noticed I'd become a more interesting guest at parties. I could carry on conversations again. No longer did drink make me disappear into the wallpaper.

After five weeks, the proverbial light came on and I saw there was an easier, softer way. By the grace of God and AA, I'm now sober more than five years. But if I hadn't drummed up a few diversions in my early recovery, I wouldn't have made it a month. In early recovery, idle time is a killer.

Years later, while chairing a meeting at my home group, it occurred to me that hobbies and outside interests might be a good topic for discussion. I thumbed through the Big Book and other AA literature looking for an entry on recovering our former pastimes as we weaned ourselves off alcohol. I found nothing.

"If you don't mind," I told the group, "I'd like to offer a topic without a companion reading. How did you spend your time in early recovery? What hobbies did you take up to replace drinking?"

It was a topic that hit a nerve. Drinking, we saw, took up a lot of time and energy, always at the expense of other things. We counted down the hours and minutes until we could pick up again. We nervously gauged our stashes and fretted over having enough to get us through a weekend. Alcohol so dominated our lives that there wasn't room for other interests. AA has restored my old interests and opened me to new ones as I've worked the Steps.

At 15 months of sobriety, my wife and I visited Santa Fe, New Mexico and stopped at the Georgia O'Keeffe Museum. To my surprise, her paintings awakened something in me. I realized I had developed a need inside for art and beauty. Even more surprising, going to the museum had been my idea. On a previous trip when I was still drinking, my wife went alone to a museum while I languished over beers.

A few months after our New Mexico trip, my pastor announced a pilgrimage to Rome. My wife urged me to go, but I was reluctant. My drunken, couch-potato days weren't far behind me and I was still a stick-in-the-mud. At length though I gave in to the idea, and returned from Italy a changed man. I broke down crying at mass in St. Peter's Basilica. The magnificent architecture took my breath away. I listened to my first opera, "The Marriage of Figaro," and was blown away.

From our hotel rooftop overlooking Rome, our music director led singalongs on his guitar. I joined in and was invited to sing with the church choir. I came home wishing I'd mastered a European language. So I hired a tutor to help revive the Spanish language skills I'd studied in high school. My next trip is to Mexico, followed by Spain.

Today, as I put on the shaving cream, I still don't recognize the man staring back at me. Who is this singing world traveler who speaks Spanish and whose dashboard speakers belt out Puccini?

Whoever he is, I like him better than the drunken bore who once dug a groove in my sofa.

Tom C.
La Salle, Illinois

In the Shadow of Mt. Kilimanjaro
April 2021

Although it seems odd to me today, prior to coming into AA I would not have been able to think of anything fun that didn't involve drinking.

I got sober in the U.S. Navy, and a year before my last drink a shipmate and I sat down at a bar and tried to come up with things we could do the following weekend without drinking. Now, who but an alcoholic would ever do such a thing? In the couple of hours we worked at it, every idea we came up with required a case of beer, a bottle of whiskey or vodka or some other alcoholic beverage. That day was a stand-out moment that I've never forgotten.

A little more than two years later, with just over a year sober, I had another memorable experience. I was on my second Western Pacific cruise (WestPac), and after 100 days underway in the Persian Gulf my ship pulled into Mombasa, Kenya. While we were there, the ship offered several organized trips, including the option of taking a one- or two-day picture-taking safari in the Tsavo East and Tsavo West wildlife preserves. I did something I would have never done on my previous drunken WestPac—I signed up to go alone on the two-day safari. It was wonderful. I took lots of photos and made so many memories that are still important to me.

On the first day of the safari, as we cruised around in minivans with pop-up tops where we could stand up and take photos, one of my fellow sailors from another ship in our task group complained the entire morning about how he should be back in Mombasa hanging out in one of the dive bars with his shipmates. This became annoying.

When our van stopped for lunch, my new friend ran off to find another shipmate who was on a one-day tour so he could trade places and go back to town that afternoon. He was not having "fun" and needed to get back to where he could just drink. I saw myself in him and knew that on my first WestPac I would have done the very same thing.

That evening our safari crew stopped at a hotel in the bush that was built on concrete columns and had hanging walkways connecting the individual hut-like rooms. It had a very nice restaurant with a viewing deck on the roof. This deck overlooked a small lake that was lit up so we could see the wild animals that came to drink there.

That night, as I was sitting under a broad, dark sky full of stars, with Mt. Kilimanjaro in the distance and drinking a wonderful cup of fresh Kenya coffee, I felt an overpowering sense of God having done for me what I could never have done for myself. I realized that my sailor friend who left at lunchtime to drink really was my former self. If I had not been sober, I would have missed this incredible experience.

Marc J.
San Diego, California

A drunk walks into a travel agency, goes up to the desk, and says, "I'd like a round-trip ticket, please."

"Where to?" the agent asks.

The drunk explains, "Why, back here, naturally."

January 2004
Alexander B.

Our Oasis
July 2016

Recently, after a long year of changes and challenges, my fiancée and I decided to take a winter vacation in Mexico. Living in Washington State can get pretty dreary between October and March, so we figured a break in December would be perfect. We could soak up a little sun, do a little shopping and finally relax.

Being the efficiency guru, and not wanting to waste a single day of vacation, I booked our outgoing flight as a red eye, leaving Washington at about 12:50 A.M. and arriving in Cancún, Mexico, around 1:30 P.M. Well, what I didn't "plan" on (insert chuckle from my sponsor) was that we would both have to get up early for work the day before and then we had a layover in Minneapolis, so we were exhausted and not exactly spiritually fit when we arrived in Cancún. Then, of course, was the sweltering, non-air-conditioned immigration and customs process. So it was 4:30 P.M. by the time we got out of the airport—35 hours later. From the airport we took a shuttle to Puerto Juárez, where we were shuffled onto a ferryboat that took us to the amazingly beautiful Isla Mujeres.

Now we felt like we were on vacation! The salty air, the crystal blue Caribbean sea, the island music…we had arrived. The island was hopping with activity, and everyone was busily entering or exiting the ferry terminal. We grabbed a taxi and headed straight to our hotel paradise. As we were checking in, the hotel clerk offered me a fruit drink from the fountain in the lobby, which I gladly accepted. Mary, thinking much quicker than me at this point, asked, "Is there alcohol in that?" The waiter, looking somewhat perplexed but smiling widely, responded, "Of course." Crisis averted.

The next day, we headed down to the beach and reef area for some sunbathing and swimming. All around us people were enjoying their fruity drinks and ice-cold beers. I was fine, though. I had my bottle of water, and besides, I had gone to my home group before I left. Later, we decided it was time to get something to eat at the hotel. At the door of the bar we were greeted by a perfect AA-like symbol painted on the cement floor.

The following day we walked around the town for a little shopping and people-watching. Feeling a little warm and seeing a gelato shop, we decided to sit down for a cone. While sitting at our table, I looked over and saw a beautifully decorated Christmas tree. It was a good reminder, because after having been on the island for a couple of days, I had completely forgotten Christmas was a week away. But it wasn't the tree that caught my eye as much as a little sign I saw just to the left of it, on the building across the plaza from where we were sitting. I said, "Mary, check this out," and she leaned over and saw what had caught my eye: it was a blue circle with a triangle in the middle.

We walked over to the building and realized we had found a little clubhouse that had English-speaking AA meetings on Mondays, Wednesdays and Fridays. It was like finding an oasis in the desert— and today was Monday! We tried to go in the doors, but they were both locked. So we decided to come back at 6:30 for the meeting.

After dinner that night, we excitedly returned ready for a meeting. It was very dark outside, except for the light that was shining from that upper room. We tried to open the doors again, but they were still locked. I stepped back a little and could see through the open window a man's head. I hollered up, "Hey!" He replied "Yeah, what can I do for ya?" "How do we get up to the meeting?" He pointed to our right and said, "You gotta take the steps." And of course, there were 12 of them. We met some wonderful people that night from many different places. Some were vacationing, some were part-time or full-time residents, but all were alcoholics, save one Al-Anon who was there to keep the rest of us straight.

Mary and I had a wonderful vacation. We snorkeled, sunbathed and visited all the sites. We shopped, we ate and we relaxed. We started our days with prayer and meditation and then just soaked in all the area offered us. We stood at the base of the pyramid temple in Chichen Itza, swam in a cenote, and marveled at the clearest starlit skies I've ever seen. It was quite a memorable trip and we are both very grateful for the little reminders that God laid out for us, the Isla Mujeres meeting, and the light that we found at the top of the steps.

Nate Y.
Chehalis, Washington

The Twelve Steps

1. We admitted we were powerless over alcohol—that our lives had become unmanageable.
2. Came to believe that a Power greater than ourselves could restore us to sanity.
3. Made a decision to turn our will and our lives over to the care of God *as we understood Him.*
4. Made a searching and fearless moral inventory of ourselves.
5. Admitted to God, to ourselves, and to another human being the exact nature of our wrongs.
6. Were entirely ready to have God remove all these defects of character.
7. Humbly asked Him to remove our shortcomings.
8. Made a list of all persons we had harmed, and became willing to make amends to them all.
9. Made direct amends to such people wherever possible, except when to do so would injure them or others.
10. Continued to take personal inventory and when we were wrong promptly admitted it.
11. Sought through prayer and meditation to improve our conscious contact with God *as we understood Him,* praying only for knowledge of His will for us and the power to carry that out.
12. Having had a spiritual awakening as the result of these steps, we tried to carry this message to alcoholics, and to practice these principles in all our affairs.

The Twelve Traditions

1. Our common welfare should come first; personal recovery depends upon A.A. unity.
2. For our group purpose there is but one ultimate authority—a loving God as He may express Himself in our group conscience. Our leaders are but trusted servants; they do not govern.
3. The only requirement for A.A. membership is a desire to stop drinking.
4. Each group should be autonomous except in matters affecting other groups or A.A. as a whole.
5. Each group has but one primary purpose—to carry its message to the alcoholic who still suffers.
6. An A.A. group ought never endorse, finance or lend the A.A. name to any related facility or outside enterprise, lest problems of money, property and prestige divert us from our primary purpose.
7. Every A.A. group ought to be fully self-supporting, declining outside contributions.
8. Alcoholics Anonymous should remain forever nonprofessional, but our service centers may employ special workers.
9. A.A., as such, ought never be organized; but we may create service boards or committees directly responsible to those they serve.
10. Alcoholics Anonymous has no opinion on outside issues; hence the A.A. name ought never be drawn into public controversy.
11. Our public relations policy is based on attraction rather than promotion; we need always maintain personal anonymity at the level of press, radio and films.
12. Anonymity is the spiritual foundation of all our traditions, ever reminding us to place principles before personalities.

AA Grapevine

AA Grapevine is AA's international monthly journal, published continuously since its first issue in June 1944. The AA pamphlet on AA Grapevine describes its scope and purpose this way: "As an integral part of Alcoholics Anonymous since 1944, the Grapevine publishes articles that reflect the full diversity of experience and thought found within the A.A. Fellowship, as does La Viña, the bimonthly Spanish-language magazine, first published in 1996. No one viewpoint or philosophy dominates their pages, and in determining content, the editorial staff relies on the principles of the Twelve Traditions."

In addition to magazines, AA Grapevine, Inc. also produces books, eBooks, audiobooks and other items. It also offers a Grapevine Complete subscription, which includes the print magazine as well as complete online access, with new stories weekly, AudioGrapevine (the audio version of the magazine), the vast Grapevine Story Archive and current online issues of Grapevine and La Viña. Separate ePub versions of the magazines are also available. For more information on AA Grapevine, or to subscribe to any of these, please visit the magazine's website at aagrapevine.org or write to:

AA Grapevine, Inc.
475 Riverside Drive
New York, NY 10115

Alcoholics Anonymous

AA's program of recovery is fully set forth in its basic text, *Alcoholics Anonymous* (commonly known as the Big Book), now in its Fourth Edition, as well as in *Twelve Steps and Twelve Traditions, Living Sober,* and other books. Information on AA can also be found on AA's website at www.aa.org, or by writing to:

Alcoholics Anonymous
Box 459
Grand Central Station
New York, NY 10163

For local resources, check your local telephone directory under "Alcoholics Anonymous." Four pamphlets, "This is A.A.," "Is A.A. For You?," "44 Questions," and "A Newcomer Asks" are also available from AA.

YOUR NEW FEELING IS THE ARTIFACT
OF A BYGONE ERA

YOUR NEW FEELING IS THE ARTIFACT OF A BYGONE ERA

CHAD BENNETT

SARABANDE BOOKS

Louisville, KY

Publisher's Cataloging-In-Publication Data

Names: Bennett, Chad, 1976– author.
Title: Your new feeling is the artifact of a bygone era : poems / Chad Bennett.
Description: First edition. | Louisville, KY : Sarabande Books, 2020
Includes bibliographical references.
Identifiers: ISBN 9781946448484 | ISBN 9781946448491 (e-book)
Subjects: LCSH: Queer theory—United States—History—Poetry.
Popular culture—United States—History—Poetry.
Celebrities—United States—History—Poetry. | LCGFT: Poetry.
Classification: LCC PS3602.E66446 Y68 2020 (print)
LCC PS3602.E66446 (e-book) | DDC 811/.6—dc23

Cover art by Harriet Horton.
Cover design by Danika Isdahl.
Interior design by Alban Fischer.

Manufactured in Canada.
This book is printed on acid-free paper.
Sarabande Books is a nonprofit literary organization.

This project is supported in part by the National Endowment for the Arts.
The Kentucky Arts Council, the state arts agency, supports Sarabande Books with
state tax dollars and federal funding from the National Endowment for the Arts.

CONTENTS

I know I've landed on a strong manuscript when I keep asking myself, as I move through the poems—*Who is she?* This was the question that stayed with me throughout *Your New Feeling Is the Artifact of a Bygone Era.* Successful poems pull us forward, deeper into their worlds, and into the mind of their maker. They fashion and preserve an idiosyncratic gravity. Who is she?

Chad Bennett, in this quietly complex and highly torqued debut, has produced an ark of queer embodiment and thought, one that is wrought with tensile clarity while holding a faithful gaze to the deeply myriad and expansive enactment of otherness. These poems stood out, not only through what they breach and reach for, but also with whom they do it. "The body is an archive," Bennett writes, and as such, here is a poetic praxis found from a library of intergenerational collaborations with Gertrude Stein, Roland Barthes, echoes of Eduardo C. Corral, Richard Siken, Maggie Nelson, Frank O'Hara, John Ashbery, and Frank Ocean. Bennett insists—through poems as varied and rich in joy and pleasure as they are complicated, dangerous, and fraught—that a writer's most tenable lineage is one he must make for himself. That to pose a queer futurity is to dismantle the canon and then carry, line by line, the inheritances of one's legacy and cultural past, including all the voices that came before us and made us possible, becoming the sum total of one's chosen family.

It is rare for a book of poems to be both rooted in a consistent thematics while also *existing*, and therefore *thriving*, as a place where these themes can live and think on the page and in the world. They declare their own truths without reducing themselves to definitives: "A bird feigns an injured wing to lure predators from its nest." Their metaphors act as epicenters, where queerness is not a category or subgenre, as it's often expected to be, but is the only bones—irreducible and undeniable—in which these poems stand. The manuscript haunted me in searing and challenging ways—the best ways—and I returned to it through the weeks, as a traveler returns to new terrain, all the while reminded that, in the end, regardless of who we are to each other, "what we have is small / and strange. But true."

—Ocean Vuong, 2018

If I had to create a god, I would lend him a "slow understanding":
a kind of drip-by-drip understanding of problems.
People who understand quickly frighten me.

—ROLAND BARTHES

It takes time to make queer people.

—GERTRUDE STEIN

First, there was faith—

                how a terrestrial

body pulled by the force of
attraction toward

              earth's molten center
nonetheless hung willing

from a fixed point.

Second, desire—

           how such a body in

and through motion could acquire a trapped
arc of momentum. . . .

1

          Then
I was born; some god

set this pendulum going

             inside me.

HOW THAT BIRD SINGS

[Ten discrete lines: four repeated]

How do you doubt your bird was untrue? Think

"Few sadder histories have been than his."

Wake late: take the boulevard soaked in sleep

Then delete his browsing history. Claim

That's just how that bird sings, just how that bird

Has his way with me where his throat begins.

Wake late: take the boulevard soaked in sleep

Where the wide turn of hair thins at his thigh

Or perk your ears at the erased tape's hiss.

Make an inkling an ambience: decide

"Few sadder histories have been than his."

How do you doubt your bird was untrue? Think

Where the wide turn of hair thins at his thigh

How the trivial fucks with the divine

[*Unpublished interview, 1962*]

I don't want to know who
the father of this movement
is. In those Shirley Temple
movies, I was so disappointed
whenever Shirley found her
father. It ruined everything.
She had been having such a
good time, tap dancing with
the local Kiwanis Club or
the newspaper men in the city
room. Those newspaper men,
who want everything ruined,
don't want to know who
ruined it. So in the city I was
a good Shirley Temple, dancing
with men in the club, or with
this local in a room in the city.

Who was it who was with
those men? Who had the time?
The city? (Was *I* in the city?)
It disappointed those in the know
who so want to know who is

7

or was or had been having who is
or was or had been dancing.
The city was a ruined temple, or
a temple of ruined time,
I don't know. Whenever I had
the time I know I was good, or
found I had been. In time,
I ruined everything. Father,
I found the movies.

That is a vapor at day's far edge. That's Lauren Bacall in a penny
arcade. That's a streaming video but will not load. That's the
static that sings, *Goodnight, dumb world.* That is a dream if it reels
or unreels. That boy's offline and 1.3 miles away. That folds itself
up into some other words. I never quite understand what you say.
"I never quite

                   understand what you say." Or that tastes like a
song lodged in my throat. That drifts like a vapor at day's far edge,
there, there where evening's rough air slips its own knot. There
there. That's that. That is just a tongue and that is no mere thing.
That can't talk to you so it bends their ears.

No blue yet. It rained
while I slept. I should
be working but
I text you your name,
three times: *You, You, You.*
Perhaps you'll come
over tonight. At my
desk I write: *The day goes
gray as weathered wood.*
It might rain again. When
you text me a picture
of yourself in front of
a mirror, masturbating,
your face obscured by
your phone, the sun blinks
on. The sky smells
of wet wool. What
is that tree called, still
and silver? I should
know. And what were you
thinking of, bored or
stirred to some joy
or stupor, fixed
on your own image
in your phone in

10

that mirror that
held your belly's burst
of shocked black hair?
What we have is small
and strange. But true.
I once thought: *to be*
in love: is to lose
face and accept it.
Isn't every poem
for someone?
Why *not* you?

How to arrange the body.

How to orient the body in relation to others or environment.

How to convey the nature of intentions and attitudes.

How to sissy that walk.

Who will write the history of the limp wrist?

The body is an archive.

The loss of even the slightest gesture is a withering of experience.

Gestures of dominance.

Gestures of bondage.

Remember the open-mouthed arc of his closed-eyes neck with your lips at the trail of his thigh.

Gestures of melancholy or foppery.

The peculiar way one enters the room.

Which room.

Joe Brainard wrote, "I remember wondering if I looked queer."

Is it gay to cross your legs at the knees?

A bird feigns an injured wing to lure predators from its nest.

Renaissance court portraits tend to portray powerful men as having swish wrists.

Yes, you look like a homo in that profile picture.

The problem has to do with: a) that gay-looking shirt, b) that gay look on your face, c) I can't tell if the arm around you is male or female but it's holding its cigarette in a gay-looking way.

What I hide with my language my body utters.

Gestures of invitation, gestures of defiance.

First, set your arm fastidiously akimbo, your palm turned back on the hip and second, keep the other limb's elbow in close so that its elevated hand sings circles in the air.

Faggy gestures.

The man I love walks like a dancer through the fey centuries, wearing his heart like a crown.

He gestures toward a painting of Napoleon entitled *The Greatest Homosexual.*

He gestures toward a kinetoscope film of a strongman nuzzling his own biceps in the rare grain of silence.

He gestures toward the party in the far room to which you have not yet arrived, to where, at the end of the hall, he will gesture toward a man arrested in 1726 for taking indecent liberties with another man, toward the posture he assumed as he avowed, "I did it because I thought I knew him, and I think there is no crime in making what I please of my own body."

POEM BEGINNING AND ENDING
WITH A LINE BY MORRISSEY

All the streets are crammed with things eager to be held—if just by
someone's eyes, just by someone's fleet dream. Take that impossible
boy clinched by a T-shirt so blue it shakes. Take the torn-up light
that he leans clean into until he feels each nerve like a word. Take
the rail bridge where, in a fever, someone has remembered to spray
today's caption—

> *HATE SOMETHING*
> *BEAUTIFUL WITH*
> *ALL YOUR HEART*

Last night I stayed up late and alone taking pictures of myself and
deleting them. In this one I front the weather in the window. In
this one I make strange in a fake leather jacket. This one I'd cringe
to describe in a poem but in this one I'm young and know how to
hurt you. O light, music, poetry, plague: in a time to come who
will remember us? for whom the only right word seems faggot,
mean mutt with the tenderest spark in its snarl, you faggot, here by
yourself in your room tonight while *all the streets are crammed with
things eager to be held.*

[New York Times Magazine, *January* 27, 2002]

Dresden was still in ruins, so we were
obliged to work twice a week clearing away
rubble around the city. We discovered
the cellars of churches and a system
of tunnels under the city. Fantastic.
It all seemed perfectly normal. We were
very happy. We made jokes. At school,
the training was quite severe, different
from schools in the West, and I enjoyed it
at first. To work around and under
the city seemed a different system
of training. We discovered it was
perfectly normal the cellars were churches;
the tunnels and rubble were schools; and the West
was away, in a fantastic clearing—
it was all perfectly normal. In ruins
we discovered work, and twice we discovered
in the work a system of jokes: so it
seemed. And the city, quite severe, seemed
perfectly happy. Still: obliged to
work in the cellars and tunnels under
the perfectly normal, we discovered

we were clearing away fantastic jokes,
and in, around, and under the jokes
we discovered—we *made*—the city under
the city, so still it seemed (at first) the first.

LIVES OF INFAMOUS MEN

History misses pansies

—Gertrude Stein

Who is a history. He is a surface the eye skims. He is not the light's scrim. He is who is. He comes in threes.

Who is a history. He misses the taste of metal. He misses the sheen of gasoline. He misses a gaped mouth and misses a gasp missing still. He unfastens history's clasp. He will not scream.

Who is a history. He will not scram. He who finds pleasure in the ledger, who anoints a fidget king, who escapes a scrape at history's edge: he.

Who is a history. Who imagines he is a history. Who is and who in imagining is. Who in a pinch. Who from scratch. Whose violet thought, freaked with jet, set adrift on history's inch.

Good morning breathing, good morning motion of the heart, time
to wake descent of food from the stomach, get up now swallowing,
hello coughing, you too yawning, hi there lust and other appetites
of the body, and when you turn, blue, to the boy in bed beside you
you think MY HEART IS A JET OF BLOOD RUN INTO THE SHAPE OF
A BIRD you think WHEN I WAS FOURTEEN THE ONLY GAY MAN
I KNEW OF CAME HOME TO A TOWN POPULATION 1,213 TO BE
WRAPPED IN HIS FAMILY'S SHAME LINED FIERCE WITH LOVE AND
THIN DOWN TO SPITTLE AND DIE you think THE GLASS ON THE
NIGHTSTAND SHIVERS AT ME you think THE NEWS OF THE MEN I
WANTED TO BECOME CAME TO ME AS OBITUARIES you think EACH
DAY MOURNING FOR A FUTURE I COULDN'T IMAGINE AND WOULD
NEVER NOW KNOW you think I FELL IN LOVE WITH A DEAD BOY I
FELL IN LOVE WITH A DEAD BOY I FELL IN LOVE WITH A DEAD BOY
over and over WITH DEAD BOYS you think I FELL IN LOVE WITH A
DEAD BOY A DEAD BOY A DEAD BOY A DEAD BOY.

19

In each shell of his torso you crawl to sleep.

So was it funny that you skulked in the stacks at the public library
reading "Please Master," horrified and hard.

So the *New York Times* thinks gay marriage is good for the economy.

So the radio told your mother you were born this way and she
believes it.

So Gertrude Stein says it takes time to make queer people.

So the air itself is one vast library
and each poem a reconstruction
of an accident that hasn't happened to you yet
and in which you met your death.

Like a keen hound a children's choir a locomotive

But how did the body veer awake but nothing I say was learned from

Or "It will be better if you just tell me"

Like a bath spreading like swollen air dimpling water

Like my matched glance, shimmering

Like whoever I was got bowled over whoever it was bowled me over

Or the residue of a chattering tub's teeth

Or air worn to honey or a faucet whistling like a

Like a station platform (as constructed in somebody's

Like a lullaby a murder ballad

Like an advancing bark

FEMMES

I was with a girl, but I felt like I was with a boy

—Violent Femmes

I was with a girl but felt like I was with a boy.

I was with a grievance but felt like I was with a blessing.

I was with a going but felt like I was with a beckoning.

I was with a grisaille but felt like I was with a blur.

I was with a grave but felt like I was with a birth.

I was with a god but felt like I was with a beast.

I was with a Genet but felt like I was with a Bataille.

I was with a grotesque but felt like I was with a beauty.

I was with a ghost but felt like I was with a body.

WHITE HALLS

[*Ten discrete lines: four repeated*]

Follow any boy down white halls to find

Or follow blue arrows to where touch maps

The small of his, the bend of his, each thing.

Be skin to sound, static to transmission.

Follow any boy down white halls to find

What the air records speaks now to me.

Be buzz to bone, be any, be none.

Wait for the swoon where the cassette's teeth catch

23

The small of his, the bend of his, each thing.

Or follow blue arrows to where touch maps

Room after room after room after room.

Begin at the end before my heart breaks.

Funny what the song in memory becomes:

Be buzz to bone, be any, be none.

LITTLE THOUGHT EXPERIMENT

I was thinking of you, or of the crease where half-light folds back the lake. Of how we feel it is stupid to be surprised. How each night: moss   windscuff   vapor   the reeds rearrange each given thing and each day wakes to a window blushing through morning's odd fog. Odd, yet the same. Your humiliation is not contagious, however fashionable to think so. You want a poem tiny enough to enclose a world of heartbreak. Instead you listen to Patsy Cline, to the lake's drowsy static at song's frayed edge, its refrain, *I don't know, I don't know, I don't know*: each time a surprise. When in this poem did *you* become *I*? Never mind how lately each morning I think *only surprise sings*, how through the window the lake unfolds, how once I couldn't think anything but you. Now the poems I love go on too long. Now it's evening. Now morning. Now there was something I wanted to say, or even sing, and now it is a long time ago, in the twentieth century, and in the next room the telephone rings.

MEMORY AND FORGETTING ARE EQUALLY ARROGANT

You were here. Then

you were a telephone wire.

Now this pane frames the sea,

how it squirms, pushes, into

then out of itself, any body

stitching its wounds shut,

stitching new wounds . . .

Ask what opens. *Your mouth.*

26   Ask what closes. *Your mouth.*

You repeatedly look aside. You have a general desire now to make each form more precise. You want to feel that the thing, as you say, has clicked. You wouldn't get back what you lost, but you might get something else. You want to distort far beyond appearance in order to recapture it. You get carried away. You excuse yourself. You prefer mostly to be alone.

You float behind a parted curtain. You are appalled by overheard conversation. You live between blows, head ringing, or you told the entire story from the start, for the third time at least. You allow a far higher proportion of your work to survive now than you did ten years ago. You are the skin of an emerging letter. You have no sense of proportion. You should propose a toast.

You speak into an imagined tape recorder, provoking the images that hound you. You would be annoyed but discreet. Your memory lapses before that face. You can't tell now which is bait, which trapped. You know it is arbitrary, that it might happen quite often, or only once. You are conscious of an emotional implication. You look around you. You open your throat to laugh.

27

what a weird-ass memory

and what does it augur oh well

now the street turns on have I been here before

where the night sparks quick against blood-pink traffic

(I was thinking of you but you never answer)

repeat the search with the omitted results included

WHERE YOUR BODY IS IS A VERY PRECIOUS PLACE

even tonight
the room
fidgets

in your
phone's
lone light

[Ten discrete lines: four repeated]

When I nodded off, I was skimming the trees

So tender in the frenzy of, menace of

Your keen T-shirt, back's curve, piano keys—

With what we know now could we want it back?

While on TV the secret century leaks

So tender in the frenzy of, menace of

My throat, tongue, my lip to testify

30   (Your paperbacks, black jacket, anxious sigh)

Like waking to the arms of a strange room

When I nodded off, I was skimming the trees

Or in the kitchen door with the party conked out

Your eyes' lines, jeans' crease, steady sway, yours

My throat, tongue, my lip to testify

While on TV the secret century leaks

∴

1. For some time now I've been wanting to write a poem about, or like, Fleetwood Mac's "Silver Springs." It would be a poem for you. You might not ever read it. I don't know if that would matter.

2. Stevie Nicks described "Silver Springs," written about the end of her relationship with Lindsey Buckingham, as a "real heartbreaker."

3. All that cloudless fall I listened to "Silver Springs" on repeat in the car but it did not let me know how to leave you.

4. Recorded for *Rumours*, although ultimately omitted from that album, "Silver Springs" ends with a long fade-out whose barely audible last lines are the refrain, "Time cast a spell on you / but you won't forget me."

5. As if to say: Time is my rival.

6. As if to say, to Time: Time, you can subdue all but a lover.

7. As if to say, to the beloved: Beloved, you can trace the reddest line through the whole wide world but when I compare you to this blue your every step will catch and drag in its terrible wake.

8. The gesture is moving but absurd, particularly since "Silver Springs" didn't appear on *Rumours* because of time: it was too long and too slow.

9. Two decades later, a second version of "Silver Springs" nonetheless enacts the first's refusal to be forgotten. This version, recorded live, became a minor hit and won a Grammy. Because it is a live recording it of course doesn't fade out, but comes instead to a firm close, followed by applause, the politeness of which is alarming after the rude menace of Nicks staring down Buckingham and keening Was I just a fool? Was I just a fool?

10. I pause the video I am streaming on YouTube to study the audience as they stupidly clap, there in 1997 and here on my phone, as if they shouldn't be hiding their faces, or at least lowering their eyes, as if they have no proper appreciation for shame.

11. Maybe I will send you the link.

12. In fact to be beautiful, shame requires only a stage.

13. In fact if people hate poetry, and mostly they do, people hate poetry because it, like humiliation, pretends but refuses to go away.

14. In fact lately I have been listening to songs, like "Silver Springs," that fade out, pretending but refusing to go away.

15. In fact the fade-out, or the technique of ending a song with a gradual decrease in volume, became common in the 1950s and reached its peak, it seems, in 1985, when the year's top ten songs featured not a single cold ending.

16. We share a space with a song, a space the song itself has created, yet at the fade-out it wanders off, a host who has mysteriously abandoned her own party, or the adults downstairs who retreat to some interior whose door edges shut and behind which we can make out the endless, outsized melody but not the words. In there someone starts sobbing, or sharply stops. In there someone is fucking, or getting fucked.

17. This is our sorrow. Once it seemed theirs, but now it's ours.
They still inhabit it, yet we say it's ours.

18. My phone is at 3%.

19. I don't know what I would say about "Silver Springs." When you were here, I would have said it to you, thinking through the queer, ongoing elsewhere of the first version's fade-out versus the puncturing now of the second's liveness. Or how, once cut from *Rumours*, "Silver Springs" was relegated to the B-side of "Go Your Own Way," Lindsey Buckingham's own, more jaunty account of the breakup with Nicks. A-side: You can go your own way. B-side: You will never get away from the sound of the woman that loves you. I might have said, Lindsey Buckingham sounds like chrome while Stevie Nicks sounds like exhaust. I might have said, That morning when I woke my body felt finally historical, there not next to any You.

20. For one blue decade I addressed myself I swear to one person only, and maybe I am still.

21. What does your half of the sky look like? Here everything is weather and far from you.

22. For some time I've wanted to write a poem called "Silver Springs," a real heartbreaker, but this is not that poem. This poem wants just to say things to you.

23. Do you know who you are?

24. And if so, then I do, too.

No cloud. No leaves
trying their reddest
in some blunt wind.
No world lit up
just so by this rain
and no rain, even.
I resolve: no more
phone calls after your
voice this morning
popped its digital
bubble and you kept
trying to talk
while I kept trying
to think *all things
are real*—cloud, leaf,
red, wind, rain, phone,
hello: why *are there*   61
no tears in this
poem? I fucking
want to cry. I think
a poem is like
Andy Warhol who
said, "I'm shy, yet
like to take up
a lot of personal

space." Days have passed
with their different
weathers. I don't know
how many times
I've rewritten these
stubbornly banal
last lines. I think
I'll respect their
banality, how what
I didn't say then
I'm saying to you
here where it matters
even less yet takes
up so much more.

I AM ODIOUS (AS IT TURNS OUT).
I AM MONSTROUS GLAD

Or, make a work out of continuously saying, in a column or list, one sentence
or line, over and over in different ways, until you get it "right"

—Bernadette Mayer

I guess we're no longer afraid of the monstrous

I guess the monstrous has no claim on us now

The monstrous I guess seeps forward like a shadow

Presses against my thigh or says shut your mouth

I can make it out in the shell of my torso

I guess my fat tongue just won't stop now

I guess the moon hangs mute in the wings of the sky

I guess this is what it feels like to be monstrous

I guess this is what it feels like to be deemed monstrous

I guess this is what it feels like to inhabit the monstrous

I guess on any crowded street there's no concealing it

I guess I thought I understood what it meant to be monstrous

I thought we would go on forever what else could we do

You say "I used to be a person now I'm a fucking ghost"

You say so this is the monstrous was it always our rival

I guess when the glass on the nightstand shivers it's shivering at me

I guess when the whole house purrs it's purring with something
    monstrous

The static so thick even if I could come back I might never find you

To say the world supplies its necessary resistance

63

To say don't be afraid who can afford it
Don't ask could it have been otherwise than monstrous how could it
If I advanced I advanced pointing to my mask
Now be delicate be fierce be shrewd I know you will
Forgive me if I remembered but too late
How a poem is just an imagined world
Where everything hoped for turns out wrong

"You are a wretched wretch," thought Pinkie. "I can't stand to hear anyone speak of you," Rose said quickly. "My throat wouldn't open, not for one word," Hale recalled. "As children we would go daily to the farthest dip of field behind our house, and practice screaming," Spicer said. Ida frowned. "I haven't let loose a good scream for years," she said. "Instead I speak, speak, speak . . . to you, and this speech makes a monster of me: all tongue." "Perhaps it is all one long soliloquy, talking to myself as if to you, to you as if myself," Pinkie thought. Cubitt began suddenly: "Near the end of that April, shortly before the events in question, I stopped off in the middle of a seemingly interminable series of errands to visit you at the pub." "We didn't know then all that would happen," interrupted Dallow. "I remember," exclaimed Rose, "how behind the counter and before a mirrored wall I stood, loafing, facing myself, and how at the sound of my name one of me turned toward you and the other away." "But look here," said Cubitt, "I don't suppose I noted this, really, until long into our timid talk, or maybe even long after, or now, just trying to, to spit this out." "It had been so long," Pinkie sighed, "I couldn't listen to what you said, and watching the three of us—you, your aloof reflection, and me—I went for some time unaware of having any body at all." Ida shuddered. "We all continued speaking, thinking our voices locked in parallel grooves. Too late we see Accident's miniscule slant."

The picture was shot before I said *smile*.
A boy. His face tight with cold. A green sea.
The camera swallowed him whole.

Salt tore hard at the white of his reach, while
the sky went blank above sea.
The picture was shot. Before I said *smile*

there was a body of water. It piled
sea-spit around his feet and licked them clean;
the camera swallowed him whole.

He knew how to love a thing: the sea wheeled
through and stained his gesture green
before the picture was shot. I said *smile*

66 *wide* at the impending waves. They now curl
into crests that never drop; they frame the scene
the camera swallowed. His whole

body was silver to me—it wanted light.
I know how to be wrong about a thing.
This picture was shot before. I said *smile*,
and the camera swallowed him whole.

The way they clutched was *our* clutch,
their hidden faces *any* face: why not
ours? It was us I saw writhing
on the surface that held me:
that I peered into, then wanted to break.

[*Ten discrete lines: four repeated*]

wish I could fall through the mirror." Granted

bared forearm and glass. The light revises

in a smoke-framed pose and swishing blue air

wish I could fall through the mirror." Granted

he held glancing toward the bar's far end

and the wine-blazoned gesture expressed there

bared forearm and glass. The light revises

68   surrogate hand that would living see to

the Hôtel des Saints-Pères: sat on the bed

in a smoke-framed pose and swishing blue air

skin shook slack or tight (perhaps) snaps, settles

note: "We all have to go, it's not so bad."

he held glancing toward the bar's far end

stilled stillness, remanence of a wish: I

PATROCLUS IN THE ARMOR OF ACHILLES

The earth what's wrong with the earth.

The sky what's wrong with the sky.

The sea, the sun, the moon, the constellations.

The wonder of cities like this city like the light glancing off of us
each as we advance or retreat like the terrible light what's wrong
with the light the people the city with beauty.

I feel like Patroclus in the armor of Achilles.

How we got here, this August Friday, what's wrong with how we
got here.

My body my body my body my train in some ten minutes.

To feel fierce at night with you walking ahead, red thread in a maze.

To feel like Patroclus in the armor of Achilles.

Is it all enormity and life will it protect me and keep me here.

In the streetlight where you walk ahead toward the train I will miss
and the cab we will catch that takes us to the room I have let where
it's so different now is it so different now.

I feel like Patroclus in the armor of Achilles.

The unbearable what's wrong with the unbearable.

The odious what's wrong with it.

The armor of Achilles what's wrong with the armor of Achilles.

but he
can't be
a man

because
he doesn't
smoke

the same
cigarettes
as me

LITTLE SPELL AGAINST FUTURE WOE

No you didn't remember the eye that held you.

No you never recognized, in odd bodies, one who saw you, creature of a moment, unwinding the unmade bed to what pressed along your neck in the back of the cab to the red of your face at the edge of some ruinous night.

No you never found yourself in that city again, didn't humiliate yourself by returning to the tawdry places.

You had no cause to have said *it is finally past* or felt its blue on your lips when once more out of time his plump fingers plucked the cherry from deep in your empty drink.

You never fooled yourself into seeing that threadbare room rich, even here, casting this spell, wherever you are, beneath basic cloud types or in the darkest of some July where no not handsomer in memory you hold his image in a shirt of rose opening to the beauty of his throat.

There was no photograph, and in that photograph the shape the light makes was not his shape, not a shadow you threw down against the days you betrayed because 1) perhaps had one too many or 2) his still air demanded your every gesture or 3) bored basically or 4) as opposed to what or 5) just self-destructive.

Nothing was different. The weathers went on into every outstretched future.

To your credit you never asked, no never said his name, when some shimmering tore at the horizon from this great distance you never even prayed, made no appeal, begging to grasp is he a boy or a beast or one thing that loves me, bent still on calling me, to strike me to sparks with the match of his voice?

Now at your lips each fleet thing recedes:
history you know is a boy asleep,
his clavicle's kiss or tonight's queer bark
thick with the spit of your chewmarked tongue
between history's teeth in the grinning dark.

History is a boy you know asleep:
you can sing his fingers' collapsed grasp,
sing hair that starts but slow at his wrist,
sing this palimpsest: forearm, sheets, slope of
his chest: *clavicula*, Latin for little

key. When it turns you know history
is a boy asleep: know his body's code
holds a century's dreams so sound their deep,
unsounded, seems the terrible pleasure

                      of being deceived.   75

EVERY KIND OF LOVE OR AT LEAST MY KIND OF LOVE
MUST BE AN IMAGINARY LOVE TO START WITH

1

Boy crouching like a hound
or small god
sniffing night's crotch

2

Boy in the heat beside
the white pool breathing
a red exhaust whose plumes
settle, still, coat each
slim limb and lazily when
he enters the water
76   spool out behind him

3

Boy at the century's
jukebox, hammered,
same furious song
on repeat

ALICE B. TOKLAS

[*The Bancroft Library Interview, 1952*]

She [Gertrude Stein] thought
at one time that
there were no more books
to read, when she was quite
young. What was she
going to do when
she got to the end
of them? And she looked
around the library
and said, "I'll get to
the end of this, and
then what?" She was young.
One was no more going
to read to the end
of books then one was
going to end time.
When she thought of this
she thought then that she
read to no end and
to end that, she was
going to read no
more. She *looked*. "I'll do
that," she said, and got

to it. She looked at
books and *read* no more.
And this was what got
the books going then.
She looked and looked and
thought of books to do
that were no more quite
books. "I'll get to *them*,"
she said, and the books
she thought of got to
them. What was this? And
what was she? One no
more thought the Library
was Time—no *were* and
was, no *then*. She (*she!*)
looked to the end when
she was no more no
more no more and the books
one read looked young.

CAUGHT IN A TRAP BUT CAN'T BACK OUT
BECAUSE I LOVE YOU TOO MUCH BABY

Remember me:
the postcard's dream

of destruction
in halls

down which all
boys flee

You found another city, better than
this one, so you threw a party and
invited the wind. The whole dumb sky
came. In the far room, did you notice?—
those were my eyes ablaze in blue chat
with some cloud I'd never met. But you had:
everyone there you'd ever known,
a leaf, scraps of light, dim hills, telephone
wire. Is it weird I wondered which ones
you'd fucked? We didn't get a chance
to talk. That's OK. Always when I walk
out into the night's amber my feelings
don't matter: "the grand scheme of things."
Scheme used to mean a diagram of all
the stuff in the sky, something to do with
scale, like my smile in the photograph
we took: just to show the vastness
around us. Should I post it? Should I
have brought you a gift? No. I almost
never think of you, whose phone I once,
in a fever I thought might never break,
broke into. Then, all I could want was
our little schemes, the things I couldn't
ask, how your glasses that like the end

80

of each day go black to starry gray would
slip, sigh at me: "Don't you know
anything?" And now I do. Lovers are stupid:
always surprised. Goodbye, you.

YOUR FADE-OUT IS A TINY PHILOSOPHY
BUT NO LESS TRUE FOR THAT

your only
teachers

are the movies
and lovers

and lovers
are like movies

only old ones
stir desire

Something I'll call *rev.*
A chirp, natural
or mechanical:
not clear. The flush
of cars that we
only hear. Wattage.
And that noise (rare)
when the weather slips
heavy and bright
into lilac and
out. To attend
to the world. To be
"needed by things."
On the phone lately
how you get me
off by talking
about past men—
like echo, a sort
of reflection, some
familiar space we
awaken like day
locked in its forgetful
pivot releases
the queer shapes each shape
can make: the broken

chair, open book, cup's
rim, empty shirt. I'm
all ears: smear, rustle,
kiss, fizz. Those sounds
were yesterday.
So far today: a mess
of wind. Hinges.

ILLEGIBLE CLOUD

[*Cy Twombly Gallery, the Menil Collection, Houston, Texas*]

Illegible cloud
in the wind's stammer
where your breath crossed me out

in the lake's spent ash
where the sky's blot bore
the leaves' fast float

and your leg against mine
in the little boat's gasp
where each letter would begin

I have tried to speak clearly

Every night fucks every day up / Every day patches the night up
—Frank Ocean

Every night fucks every day up; every day patches the night up.

Every word fucks every sentence up and every sentence seals the words up.

I know how the outer weather can fuck up the inner, and the inner weather can fuck up the outer.

And certain skies have fucked with this one, whose every cloud swells replete with those.

Every kiss scars a throat and every throat heals the kiss still ice-sharp at the base of each neck.

I searched for a GIF to show in time-lapse every moon-blooming flower opening onto worlds that narrow to a light-latched close.

I took a photo of you that like all the others fucked up the beauty of your each little gesture.

Like every air tarnishes this morning's silver.

Every shadow's maw, or eye's amber, or fleet blast of sun, or what could disguise my hunger.

Every digital glitch, every marginal jot, every jizzed sheet, every fresh-combed part.

All that spoils in every pleasure pleasures every spoiled life.

Every day, every night, every day, every night.

: : :
: : :

YOUR NEW FEELING IS THE ARTIFACT
OF A BYGONE ERA

how it
becomes
birdsong

if we
cut out
its tongue

The poems in this book assemble, absorb, contend with, and perform an idiosyncratic archive of voices, objects, and ephemera, the following among them.

The epigraph from Roland Barthes can be found in the publication of his 1977–1978 lecture course on *The Neutral*, translated by Rosalind E. Krauss and Denis Hollier. The epigraph from Gertrude Stein can be found in her 1925 novel *The Making of Americans.*

The title of "Idiorrhythmy" refers to Roland Barthes's notion of a form of being together that recognizes individual rhythms of life: the fantasy of living together, but according to each subject's own rhythm. Barthes sets out these ideas in his 1976–1977 lecture course, translated by Kate Briggs and published as *How to Live Together: Novelistic Simulations of Some Everyday Spaces.*

The opening line of "How That Bird Sings" revises the final line of Emily Dickinson's 1865 poem "Split the Lark—and you'll find the Music—" (Johnson #861): "Now, do you doubt that your Bird was True?" The repeated line "Few sadder histories have been than his" appears in a brief obituary for Oscar Wilde published in the *Literary World*, December 7, 1900.

The opening lines of "Andy Warhol" are taken from an originally unpublished interview with Warhol, conducted in 1962 and 1963 by David Bourdon. The transcript was not printed until 2004, when it appeared in *I'll Be Your Mirror: The Selected Andy Warhol Interviews*.

The lines *"to be / in love: is to lose / face and accept it"* in "'Trick" are adapted from the published version of Roland Barthes's 1978–1979 and 1979–1980 lecture course, *The Preparation of the Novel*, translated by Kate Briggs.

"Some Faggy Gestures" takes its title from a 2008 artist's book of the same name by Henrik Olesen that both documents his visual installations and expands upon them through the artist's text. The quotation attributed to Joe Brainard is from his 1975 book *I Remember*. The line "What I hide with my language my body utters" is adapted from Roland Barthes's *A Lover's Discourse: Fragments* (1978), translated by Richard Howard. The 1964 painting *The Greatest Homosexual* is by Larry Rivers. The poem's final sentence adapts the response of William Brown, as reported in the trial proceedings of the Old Bailey, after being entrapped and arrested in England in 1726 for "an Intent to commit Sodomy."

"Poem Beginning and Ending with a Line by Morrissey" begins and ends with a line from the Smiths' 1983 song "Handsome Devil."

The opening lines of "Gerhard Richter" are taken from a statement of Richter's that appears in "An Artist Beyond Isms*by Michael Kimmelman, from the January 27, 2002 *New York Times Magazine*.

"Lives of Infamous Men" shares its title with Michel Foucault's 1977 essay introducing the unfinished series *Parallel Lives*, a projected anthology drawn from the prison archives of the Hôpital général de Paris and the Bastille. The poem's epigraph is from Gertrude Stein's 1930 poem "A French Rooster. A History." The final lines invoke John Milton's *Lycidas* (1637): "the pansy freaked with jet, / The glowing violet."

"B L U E" echoes Anohni's 2001 song "I Fell in Love with a Dead Boy" (recorded as Antony and the Johnsons). "Please Master" refers to the 1968 poem by Allen Ginsberg. The song on the radio is, unfortunately, Lady Gaga's "Born This Way" (2011). The poem's final lines adapt the title of a 1969 artwork by Christian Boltanski, *Reconstitution d'un accident qui ne m'est pas encore arrivé et où j'ai trouvé la mort.*

The epigraph to "Femmes" is from the Violent Femmes' 1986 song "I Held Her in My Arms."

The Patsy Cline song alluded to in "Little Thought Experiment" is "Then You'll Know" (1957, written by Bobby Lile).

The title of "Memory and Forgetting Are Equally Arrogant" is borrowed from Roland Barthes's *The Neutral.*

"Theory of the Lyric" is titled after Jonathan Culler's 2015 study *Theory of the Lyric.*

"Soon-to-Be Innocent Fun / Let's See" shares its title with a 1986 song by Arthur Russell.

"Where Your Body Is Is a Very Precious Place" takes its title from a statement by Edith Ewing Bouvier Beale, or Big Edie, in the documentary film *Grey Gardens* (1975, directed by Albert Maysles, David Maysles, Ellen Hovde, and Muffie Meyer): "I'm not ashamed of anything. Where my body is is a very precious place."

"Silver Springs" is for Ashly Bennett. The poem's third part alludes to the final lines of Frank O'Hara's 1959 poem "Les Luths." The poem's fifteenth part draws on William Weir's essay "A Little Bit Softer Now, a Little Bit Softer Now . . . : The Sad, Gradual Decline of the Fade-Out in Popular Music," published online in *Slate* on September 14, 2014.

The title of "How to Live Together" is borrowed from Roland Barthes's lecture course *How to Live Together*. The quotation attributed to Andy Warhol is adapted from his 1975 book *The Philosophy of Andy Warhol (From A to B and Back Again)*. The poem responds in part to Robert Frost's adage, from his 1939 essay "The Figure a Poem Makes," "No tears in the writer, no tears in the reader."

The epigraph to "I Am Odious (As It Turns Out). I Am Monstrous Glad" is from Bernadette Mayer's list of writing experiments.

"*Brighton Rock*" borrows its title and dramatis personae from Graham Greene's 1938 novel of the same name.

The title of "Punctum" names Roland Barthes's concept, elaborated in *Camera Lucida: Reflections on Photography* (1980, translated by Richard Howard in 1981), of the aberrant detail of a photograph that pricks or wounds the observer, attracting and holding their gaze.

The title of "George Dyer" refers to the painter Francis Bacon's lover, who took an overdose of sleeping pills and was found dead in their hotel bathroom two days before the opening of Bacon's major 1971 retrospective at the Grand Palais in Paris. The poem quotes a note left by Dyer before a previous suicide attempt, while on holiday with Bacon in Greece: "We all have to go, it's not so bad."

"Patroclus in the Armor of Achilles" borrows and revises a line from Frank O'Hara's 1959 poem "Joe's Jacket": "It is all enormity and life it has protected me and kept me here."

"The Homosexual Tradition in American Poetry" shares its title with a foundational 1979 study by Robert K. Martin, and repurposes lyrics from the Rolling Stones' 1965 song "(I Can't Get No) Satisfaction."

The last lines of "Now at Your Lips" adapt a principle voiced by Lady Stutfield in Oscar Wilde's 1893 play *A Woman of No Importance*: "The secret of life is to appreciate the pleasure of being terribly, terribly deceived."

"Every Kind of Love or At Least My Kind of Love Must Be an Imaginary Love to Start With" takes its title from the opening lyrics of Rufus Wainwright's 1998 song "Imaginary Love."

The opening lines of "Alice B. Toklas" are taken, as noted, from a 1952 interview conducted for the University of

California, Berkeley's Bancroft Library. Toklas's interviewer was Robert Duncan.

The title of "Caught in a Trap but Can't Back Out Because I Love You Too Much Baby" is adapted from Elvis Presley's 1969 song "Suspicious Minds," written by Mark James.

The opening line of "Goodbye Party" adapts the second line of C. P. Cavafy's 1894 poem "The City," as translated by Edmund Keeley. The final lines rework, from experience, Roland Barthes's assertion in *A Lover's Discourse* that "what is stupid is to be surprised. The lover is constantly so."

The title of "The Noise of Time Is Not Sad" is borrowed from a statement in Roland Barthes's *Camera Lucida*. The poem references Frank O'Hara's declaration, in his 1954 poem "Meditations in an Emergency," that "I am bored but it's my duty to be attentive, I am needed by things."

"Illegible Cloud" responds, in part, to viewing Cy Twombly's 1994 painting *Untitled (Say Goodbye, Catullus, to the Shores of Asia Minor)* in the Menil Collection's Cy Twombly Gallery.

The title and epigraph of "Nights" are from Frank Ocean's 2016 song "Nights." This poem and this book are for Manny Alcala, every day, every night.

ACKNOWLEDGMENTS

Not without the editors of the following publications in whose pages some of these poems first appeared: *Borderlands, BafterC* (Book*hug Press), *Colorado Review, Columbia Review, Denver Quarterly, Fence, fields, Figure 1, Free Verse: A Journal of Contemporary Poetry and Poetics, Gulf Coast, jubilat, Likestarlings, The Offing, OmniVerse, Poetry Daily, Verse Daily,* and *The Volta.*

Not without Harriet Horton's kind permission to use the image of her art that appears on the cover.

Not without the generous words of Eduardo C. Corral and D. A. Powell and the queer space their work has created.

Not without the gift of Ocean Vuong's foreword and his being with these poems.

Not without Sarah Gorham and her brilliant squad at Sarabande— Kristen Miller, Danika Isdahl, and Joanna Englert, as well as Alban Fischer and Emma Aprile—who have made, with insight and care, this book a thing in the world.

Not without Ashly Bennett.

Not without Manny Alcala.

Not without my family, friends, lovers, teachers: intimate or strange, dead or living, each who tried and tries, even now, to show stupid me, one way or another, how.

CHAD BENNETT is the author of *Word of Mouth: Gossip and American Poetry*, a study of twentieth century poetry and the queer art of gossip. He currently lives in Austin, Texas, where he is an associate professor of English at the University of Texas at Austin. This is his first book of poems.

SARABANDE BOOKS is a nonprofit literary press located in Louisville, KY. Founded in 1994 to champion poetry, short fiction, and essay, we are committed to creating lasting editions that honor exceptional writing. For more information, please visit sarabandebooks.org.